WHERE THE
ACTION
IS

WHERE THE ACTION IS

STEPHEN W. BROWN

FLEMING H. REVELL COMPANY
OLD TAPPAN, NEW JERSEY

Scripture quotations in this volume are from the *Revised Standard Version of the Bible*, Copyrighted 1946 and 1952, unless otherwise identified.

Scripture quotations identified KJV are from the *King James Version of the Bible.*

SBN-8007-0430-4 cloth
SBN-8007-0443-6 paper

TO the women in my life:
my mother Launia,
my wife Anna
and my daughters
Robin and Jennifer

Contents

Preface
1 The Minister   13
2 The Christ   29
3 The Church   50
4 The World   71
5 The Task   90
6 The Future   110

Preface

I AM A YOUNG MINISTER. If you're like a lot of other people, you probably think I'm somehow different and strange: either I'm a neuter personality who loves everybody and talks about God, or I'm angry and radical. The truth is that I'm not neuter; I don't love everybody; I talk about lots of things, and my anger and radicalism are usually reserved for those who think I am neuter, loving, and godly.

I am in the ministry for a reason. I have discovered something real and wonderful in Jesus Christ, and He wants me here. My God is not dead; the Church of Jesus Christ through which I serve is not dying, and I am not ashamed of either.

I write this book from the perspective of a young man just beginning his ministry, and I would ask forgiveness from those who will see in it an obvious lack of experience and years. I just feel that so much is being written these days about either the "sweet, smiling young parson" or the "new, radical young clergyman" that I want to show another picture. I want to explain the faith of one young man who allows himself to be called "Reverend" when he knows he isn't.

STEPHEN W. BROWN

WHERE THE
ACTION
IS

1

THE MINISTER

I have appeared unto thee for this purpose, to make thee a minister and a witness both of these things which thou hast seen, and of those things in the which I will appear unto thee.

ACTS 26:16 KJV

A DITCHDIGGER knows his job is to dig ditches; he knows how deep, how wide, and how long his ditch should be. He knows, if he takes the time to ask, the reason for the ditch. If he has been digging ditches very long he should have some idea of the tools he will need, and when he finishes his work he can look back on it and say, "I dug that ditch."

However, it is not that simple for a minister. Each year many men leave seminaries and the ordained ministry because they found the long hard ecclesiastical road went in a direction other than the one they had planned. As I look over some of my own conceptions of the ministry, I see a complex mixture of spiritual advisor, prophetic preacher, skilled administrator, and loved pastor. But if I am honest with myself, I will know that most of the time I am not spiritual enough to advise anyone, that I don't want to pay the price of a prophet, that my administrative plans often look like Jericho after the trumpets, and that I am not so much a loved pastor as a tolerated cleric. The tasks for which I have been called are so far beyond me and my talents that it is downright frightening. Preacher, psychologist, administrator, prophet, evangelist, marriage counselor, pastor, and teacher are only a few of the tasks I see before me. Every day of my life there will be a feeling of having failed in an important facet of my calling. There will be many times when, unlike the ditchdigger, I won't be able to look back and say, "I did that, and I am glad." I won't be able to say it because I won't be able to see what I have done.

It's very hard for a young man, at the beginning of his ministry, to identify with this typical pastoral image. Most parishioners believe their minister is far above the average man in matters spiritual. They believe he has a personal line to God, and he can rear back and perform a miracle almost anytime he's inclined. Because he is in deep, personal, dynamic communication with God, he can tell them anything they need to know about Him, or how to pray to Him, or how to have faith in Him. After all, they say, the minister has studied theology and the Bible and philosophy, so he ought to know.

The trouble with this myth is that too many ministers believe it. They have been held up by others as a substitute for God for so long that they have come to believe they are God or at least a reasonable facsimile of Him. In just the short time I have been in the ministry I have been told so many times that I was godly, spiritual, dynamic, and saintly that, had it not been for an honest wife and a God who doesn't mind punching holes in inflated egos, I would have believed it far longer than I did.

It is easy for a man to look saintly. It is not really difficult to talk with a stained-glass voice about God, and anyone who has tried knows that one can quote theologians, philosophers, and eminent writers with very little effort. However, it is another matter to tell people that you aren't the saintly person they thought you to be. It is difficult to be honest about human needs, human problems, and human fears, especially when people think you don't have any.

A friend of mine who has been married to a minister for almost ten years met a former classmate of hers at a class reunion. During the course of conversation my friend mentioned that she had married a minister. A look of horror crossed the other woman's face, and in a voice dripping with sympathy she said, "Oh, I'm so sorry—sex is so wonderful." That says something disturbing about the minister's image, and the saddest thing about it is ministers often helped to create it. It is no accident that most movies, plays, and novels portray ministers as sexless, anemic half-saints who would be out of place at anything other than a ladies-aid social, dressed in anything other than a black suit.

When a minister is confronted by his own misconceived self-image, he can pursue his ministry in any one of three ways.

If he suffers from the illusion that he is what he and others think he is, he can become the "answer man." He can feel that because he has superior training in the field of religion, it must follow that he has superior answers to all questions. He can rule his Elders, his official Board, his Church Council, his Trustees, or his Deacons with the attitude that he is the one man to whom all questions of any importance should be addressed. When there are problems in the church, it will be because "the laymen are just not intelligent or sophisticated enough to understand." When the church can't meet its bills, it will be because "the laymen are not interested enough in God's work to pay their pledges." When the attendance is down and the empty pews reflect the light behind the pulpit, it will be because the "laymen are not witnessing." When the people begin to leave the church, it will be because "they can't hear the truth." And when the minister is criticized, it will be because the "laymen can't see greatness when it stares them in the face."

This attitude gives many laymen the feeling that a minister is off in a world by himself, a judgment which is quite often true. The loneliness many ministers suffer is not always the loneliness of the prophet but rather the loneliness of one who has walled himself off in an ivory tower of answers to questions no one asks. How sad it is to see such a man come to the end of his ministry in a church and say, "I told them the truth, but no one listened." To play the role of God is terribly dangerous business for anyone, and especially for the minister.

Before we look at the second way a minister may be affected by his identity problem, let us say that there *are* ministers who *do* suffer from the loneliness of the prophet. Many men have been removed from their pulpits because they told the truth, because they were faithful, because they decided it was more important to please God than their congregation. The minister who has never had to hold on to the sides of his pulpit to brace himself against the storm caused by speaking God's Word just isn't worth his salt—and most ministers

16

are. The point is there are far fewer persecuted prophets than there are those who say they are.

Sometimes a minister can clearly distinguish the differences between what he would like to be, what others think he is, and what he really is. Then he can either leave the ministry or try to live with the inconsistency. I had a friend in seminary who told me he was thinking of leaving the ministry, and when I asked him why he said, "I just didn't know what was expected of me. I can't live a lie." At the time I didn't understand my friend's feelings. In fact, I spent most of that day telling him why he shouldn't leave. However, during the few years I have been serving a church, I have come to understand what he meant. How often I have been writing a sermon that would be just the thing Mr. Jones needed, only to realize it was just the thing Steve Brown needed. When I have talked about prayer, I have often been forced to see the inadequate state of my own prayer life. When I have spoken about the necessity of commitment to Christ, I have had to face up to my own lack of commitment. When I have spoken out about social issues, I have had to examine my own lack of action. Whenever I have preached to others, I have been forced to tears by the realization that I must say "we" and not "you." Because of these inconsistencies, it is easy to leave the ministry for a profession where one does not have to feel the sting of hypocrisy.

So often, when people place me on a spiritual pedestal, I am tempted to say to myself, "Of course, they're wrong to place me in such a position. But it does make me feel good, so I'll just keep quiet about it." And soon I find myself living so as to receive the praise of those who would keep me on the pedestal. I am judging myself in terms of what other people think, rather than what I know to be true. After a while, I learn to live with the inconsistencies and perhaps even to like them. It is this road which leads a minister into the life of an actor playing a part to please the crowd, and it is a superficial, empty, frustrating part he plays.

Now if these were the only alternatives, then I would have to leave the ministry. But there is another way that perhaps most older ministers have known for a long time. I am just learning.

A minister can let others in on the secret that he is human. He can look at his own misconceived self-image, and the mistaken image he is given by others, and he can be honest with himself and with them. He can admit his inadequacies and failures. He can say to the people to whom he ministers, "Look, I know about your fear, your hurt, your loneliness, and your sin because I, too, am afraid, lonely, and hurt. I also am a sinner." Then he can become, as the late Daniel T. Niles has stated in his book *That They May Have Life*, "only a beggar telling another beggar where to find food." Therein lies the only path a minister can take with honesty and integrity. This is what Christ meant when He called Paul into the ministry and said, "I have appeared unto thee for this purpose, to make thee a minister and a witness both of these things which thou hast seen and of those things in the which I will appear unto thee" (Acts 26:16 KJV).

I am learning to see myself at the beginning of my ministry as only a witness to those things which I have seen, and to those things which Jesus Christ will cause me to see in the future. It is a unique kind of witness in

18

that I have been called by God to be a minister and ordained by His Church to "care for God's church" (I Timothy 3:5). However, in its basic form my ministry must be, as it must also be for the layman, only a witness to a reality I have encountered and known for myself, a witness to the faith that is within me, a witness to something other than myself— something I know to be true in my own life and experience.

When I examine my own faith, no matter how small and weak I can see certain real and vital things. I have experienced forgiveness. I have experienced a Power other than myself. I have experienced the awe of standing before a holy God. I have known the reality of being accepted by Jesus Christ. In my encounter with Him I have known love, understanding, meaning, and healing. When I have stood in His presence I have seen that I can never avoid my responsibility to others and remain in His presence. Furthermore, I have experienced these things in a depth and reality I have found nowhere else. It is to all this that I must become a witness.

If I choose this way to make my ministry relevant, I will be freed from the necessity to make others think I am perfect. I can talk about hate because I have hated. I can talk about lust because it is real in my own life. I can talk about pride and selfishness because they are old adversaries. But most of all, I can talk about a God who has come to me in spite of my sins, who has loved me even when He knew me, and who has made me clean even knowing how unclean I am. When I stand on Calvary knowing the kind of person I am and seeing the kind of love God is, I am overwhelmed with "the wonder of it all." Paul's words become mine, "The saying is sure and worthy of full acceptance, that Christ Jesus came into the world to save sinners. And I am the foremost of sinners..." (I Timothy 1:15 KJV). Therein is my message.

Recently, a young woman who is in her freshman year of college came to me with a great burden of guilt. I don't know what she expected of me. Perhaps she wanted to find someone who would help her rationalize; perhaps she wanted someone who was perfect to tell her how to be perfect; maybe she was just looking for someone who would listen. She began by confessing to me her great sin, and then she asked me what to do.

For once I didn't talk about how good I was. I didn't talk about the need to change herself. I didn't even give her some friendly pastoral advice on the art of living. Rather, very simply I tried to tell her about my own experience. I told her that no matter what she had heard about ministers, we were just as prone to sin as anyone else. And then I introduced her to Jesus who promised help, healing, and forgiveness.

I must confess that when I told her these things I did so with much "fear and trembling." You see I had for once come out from behind my ecclesiastical wall of dishonesty, and it was pretty frightening territory. Two Sundays later I was preaching a sermon on Christian joy. After the service, this particular young lady came to me with tears in her eyes. She said, "Two weeks ago I would not have known what you were talking about. Now I do for the first time in my life."

That experience taught me a lesson. It taught me that I do have a message which can change, renew, heal, and cleanse. My trouble had been that I was not being honest about the message. I had been so busy being a witness to myself that I had failed to be a witness to the only thing which was important. When I saw this problem, my whole ministry took on new meaning. Meetings in the church came alive for me because I no longer had to play a part. The pulpit became an exciting place because I no longer had to hide behind it. And above all, the people of my church began to listen, because for a change I wasn't talking about Steve Brown, but about Jesus Christ —and Jesus did have the answers.

Of course, all this presupposes certain points. It presupposes that I have encountered Christ in my life, that I have something to which I can be a witness, and that there is a relationship behind my religion. Without at least this much I am really a hypocrite.

There was once a man who wanted to be a lion trainer. He went to the public library and asked the librarian for a good book on lion training. The man studied the book until he could quote most of it from memory. Armed with his new knowledge, one night he went to the local zoo and climbed into the lion cage, and found himself face-to-face with the object of his emotions. But alas! The lion ate him up. Just so in the ministry, knowledge and training are necessary, but without the experience of being with Jesus, the knowledge and training will get us eaten. Empty words, worn-out phrases, and pious platitudes are not enough when you are speaking to a tired world grown sick of the phony.

What I am trying to say and what I have found to be true is this: it is easy to witness to a religion. A lot of us do that. But Christianity is not a religion. It is a wonderful, dynamic, revolutionary relationship with Jesus Christ. There is a big difference.

When a minister talks, he can say, "I know a creed; let me tell you about it," and no one will listen. He can say, "I'm about the best minister going; let me tell you about me," and he will be ignored. But if he says, "I have been with Jesus; let me tell you about Him," he will have a witness that will turn the world up-side-down.

Paul said, " . . . you show that you are a letter from Christ . . . written not with ink but with the Spirit of the living God . . . " (II Corinthians 3:3). That is the description of a relevant minister of Jesus Christ.

The concept of the minister becoming an honest witness is easier to understand and accept than to put into practice. I know from experience how easy it is to create the self-illusion of being God's gift to the church, of having all the answers, of seeing laymen as "Junior Christians" sitting at my feet. I can think this way and think I am honest. But being honest and thinking I am honest are different things. As a minister I must find a way to keep honesty real and reality honest. This is especially true for the young minister because he can fool himself for just so long before it becomes too late to change. Ways get set, patterns become rigid, and soon the actor doesn't remember anything but the part.

There are three places where the Christian can find the priceless pearl of honesty.

The first source is from God, and one grasps that only in prayer. I have found, and only recently, that there is a direct correlation between the depth and quality of a minister's prayer life and his usefulness in God's service.

The times when my ministry fell apart, when my church seemed to be going in the wrong direction because I was leading it, when all my efforts seemed hollow and empty, were precisely the times when I didn't have the time nor the desire to pray.

I am very grateful to my seminary for teaching me theology, philosophy, administration, and pastoral psychology, but nobody took the time to teach me how to pray nor even to tell me how important it was. As a result, I got the idea that the problems confronting a minister could be resolved with theology, philosophy, administration, and pastoral psychology. They can't. Whenever I tried to play the role of boy psychologist or junior theologian I made the problems worse. I have found the three most important prerequisites for effective ministry are prayer, prayer, and prayer.

My teachers in seminary told me I ought to spend at least one hour of preparation for every minute I spend in the pulpit. The formula is a good one if it includes fifteen minutes of study and forty-five minutes of prayer.

If a minister is serious about his ministry and about prayer, one of the recurrent themes in his prayer life will be the quest for honest self-knowledge. My one great obstacle to effectiveness in the ministry is myself. My pompous judgmental attitude, my anger, my need for praise, my lack of love, my rationalization, my pride were all things I couldn't see until I prayed for God to reveal anything in my life that was contrary to Him. When I prayed for self-knowledge, I didn't realize what I was asking. For the first time, I began to look at myself in the cold hard light of reality, and it was frightening. All the time I thought I was being honest, pure, and good, I was just the opposite.

God has a unique way of shattering our oversized egos if we want Him to, and it is necessary for Him to do it daily. It is not an easy process, but necessary for any Christian who wants to become an effective witness to his Lord. Our deadness through our own sin is always in the way. Mother Basilea Schlink, in her tremendously penetrating book *Repentance—The Joy-Filled Life*, has said it well, "Only those who are alive can bring life to others. Dead people are unable to reproduce life by word or deed. They are simply dead. But the repentant one is full of divine life and able therefore, to beget it in others. When he says, 'I have sinned, I am guilty,' lying prostrate before God and man with a broken heart, his words have life. They open the hardest hearts and bring life to the dead. These words spoken by the prodigal son, as he lay weeping before his father, caused the father's heart to overflow with love. These words spoken now before men open their hearts for forgiveness. Tears of contrition soften the most unforgiving hearts, creating in them love and new life."

The second source of honesty is Scripture. Many Christians read the Scriptures only for comfort and guidance, and certainly this is laudable. But of equal importance is the power of Scripture to convict the Christian, to keep him honest with himself and with others. To read Scripture for guidance and comfort without also looking for a criterion against which life can be measured is like reading a weight-watcher's guide without dieting.

Scripture through the Holy Spirit is a sword which can cut through our empty piousity and phony goodness, if we will only let it teach us about ourselves. A minister ought always to be searching Scripture, not only for sermon material or theological proof texts or justification for doubtful actions, but for a faithful reflection of himself. Let me give you an illustration of what I mean. I suppose I had read the story of Abraham being willing to offer Isaac as a sacrifice a hundred times (Genesis 22). Each time I saw something different but never anything related to me. For instance, in church school as a child I thought this was an exciting story. During the pseudo-sophisticated period of my life, when I fancied myself an agnostic, I saw in this story a confirmation of my suspicions that the Bible taught child sacrifice. Later, when I entered seminary, I saw in the same passage of Scripture a good illustration of the Graf-Wellhausen documentary hypothesis. This story (for some strange reason known only to the professor) was important as an example of the Elohist documents. When I started serving my first church, the story became a text to be used as a jump-off point for a sermon or commitment. However, recently this story has been used by God to show me I have a lot of Isaacs in my own life; I have held many things, such as ecclesiastical status and theological knowledge, above my obedience to Him. I have been shown that even these must be offered on the altar, just as Abraham was willing to offer Isaac, his beloved son.

Of course, many more examples could be offered. The point is this: any Christian, including the minister who doesn't find in Scripture enough words to keep him humble has not been reading Scripture properly. Any minister who gives the impression from the pulpit that he is judging his congregation's sins without judging his own will give the impression either that he is "super-Christian" and possibly remote from their experiences, or, for those who know him better, that he is a hypocrite. One of the ways a minister can avoid both is to keep the demands of Scripture constantly before himself.

(1) The final way a minister can keep himself honest is perhaps the hardest way, for it involves other people. It is the ability to accept and utilize the criticism of others. I have found most ministers, including myself, are highly defensive when they hear anything that even approaches criticism of themselves. How could anyone question a man of God? Then immediately we begin to defend ourselves. But often this criticism has come from God by way of others, and it would behoove us to listen to it.

Some typical statements made by ministers in reaction to criticism are: "I don't know who they think I am, but I am not their hired servant." "They expect me to hold their hands when they ought to be out holding someone else's hand." "If she calls me one more time, I'm going to tell her exactly what I think." "I don't know who he thinks he is, telling me my sermon ought to be put on the bottom of the stack." "The gall of Mrs. Jones telling me I'm not doing enough visiting; doesn't she know I have to have some time to myself?" "If they don't like the way this job is being handled, let them do it."

While not all of the above reactions refer to criticism that is just, they all show a defensive attitude, indicating that the person who made them may have been hit with at least a degree of truth. The fact the statements were made at all ought to give those who made them some cause for self-examination. In fact, we can gauge the quality of our lives by our reaction to criticism, even when that criticism is unjust. I have a minister friend who was once criticised for dishonesty by one of his parishioners. The criticism was unjust; however, my friend's reaction was in itself highly revealing. Had he responded with a who-does-she-think-she-is statement, there is at least a possibility he might have had doubts about his honesty. My friend's reaction, however, was one of nondefensive openness, which in itself spoke for his honesty. Defensiveness should play no part in the life of any Christian, especially the minister. It is a sign we care more what others think of us than what they think of our Lord.

What about the times when the criticism is just? Anyone who has been a minister very long knows that some parishioners can be very critical. (I have one minister friend whose wife was criticized because her dress didn't match the curtains in the church.) Nevertheless, a minister ought to listen to criticism very carefully. More often than not he will find at least some truth in it, and when he does he ought to thank God. If he doesn't change because of the criticism, at least he will be aware of the need for change which in itself is quite a step down from the "ecclesiastical pedestal."

As I begin my ministry, I want to be faithful. I want to be fruitful. I want to be dedicated. But most of all I want to be honest in my witness and my relationship with Jesus. I want to say, with Paul, "Therefore, having this ministry by the mercy of God, we do not lose heart. We have renounced disgraceful, underhanded ways; we refuse to practice cunning or to tamper with God's word, but by the open statement of the truth we would commend ourselves to every man's conscience in the sight of God" (II Corinthians 4:1–2). That is the best gift a minister can give the people to whom he ministers.

2

THE CHRIST

*Abide in me, and I in you. As the branch
cannot bear fruit by itself, unless it abides in the
vine, neither can you, unless you abide in me. I
am the vine, you are the branches. He who
abides in me, and I in him, he it is that bears
much fruit, for apart from me you can do nothing.*

John 15:4–5

IF YOU COULD take from Christianity its clergy, its church
buildings, its creeds, its doctrines, its ritual, and its programs, what would be left? In other words, what lies at the
very heart of the Christian faith? One would think a young
man entering the ministry ought to know the answer to
those questions. After all, he is going to be a "professional"
Christian and a professional ought to know at least the
nature of his business. But, as unbelievable as it may sound,
I was already in seminary and serving as a student pastor
before I learned the nature of Christianity. Not only that,
I didn't learn it at the feet of a seminary professor nor from
an ecclesiastical text book. In fact, I did not learn it at all;
I experienced it.

My misconceptions had been many. For instance, there
was a time when I thought the essence of Christianity was

morality. If you obeyed a prescribed moral code, you were a Christian, and if you didn't you weren't. To be good was to be Christian and to be Christian was to be good. I suppose it was only natural for me to view Christianity from this perspective considering the fact most other Americans accepted the same view. It is a part of the American folk religion.

I figured that since I was going to be a minister I had to be especially good, righteous, loving, kind, honest, and honorable. There were certain things I had to do (e.g. pray, read the Bible, sing hymns), and there were certain things I ought not to do (e.g. smoking, drinking, cursing, lying). The problem came when I tried to live up to the code. No matter how much I tried, no matter how hard I worked at it, I was just not as good, pure, righteous, loving, kind, honest, and honorable as I ought to have been. Not only that, most of the time I was just the opposite. Every morning I would pray, "Today, Lord, I'm going to be the kind of person You will be proud of; today is the day I'm really going to be Christian." And then at night I wouldn't be able to sleep because of the guilt.

Paul knew that kind of guilt, too. He said, "I do not understand my own actions. For I do not do what I want, but I do the very thing I hate. . . . For I do not do the good I want, but the evil I do not want is what I do (Romans 7:15–19).

Not too long ago a popular song described an automobile accident in which the singer's girl friend had been killed. Throughout the song the singer repeats the refrain that he has to be good so he can go to heaven and be with his girl friend when he dies. Well, if heaven is peopled with those who are good enough to get there, it will be an empty place, and if the young man who sang the song "put all of his marbles in that bag," he found out just how miserable a person can be. I used to separate people into two categories: the *good guys* (they were the Christians) and the *bad guys* (they weren't). After only a short time in the ministry I know now there aren't *good guys* and *bad guys*, only bad ones who know it, and bad ones who don't know it. The Psalmist put it this way, "They have all fallen away; they are all alike depraved; there is none that does good, not one" (Psalms 53:3).

Recently I was talking to a man about becoming a Christian. He knew his life was miserable and empty; he knew how much he needed to find God. He then told me the reason he didn't become a Christian was because he didn't think he was good enough. How wrong he was! It was good news to him when he discovered the first step toward becoming a Christian is realizing one is not good enough. How many people never take that first step because someone (most likely a minister) has communicated the mistaken idea that a Christian is a morally superior person. That is not Christianity; it is the American folk religion, and it doesn't work. It doesn't work because it isn't true.

There was a time when I thought the essence of Christianity was its way of getting a moral outlook accepted by the general public. In other words, I saw Christianity as a political philosophy. I suppose this idea began to develop in seminary when I noticed most of my friends and most of my professors were adherents of a certain political outlook, usually liberal. In times past it has been conservative. To be Christian was to support certain

31

legislation, to endorse certain candidates, and (if you happen to be a minister) to preach "issue oriented" sermons. If you were leaning to the left, Jesus became a revolutionary, and if you were leaning to the right, Jesus was anti-Communist. The goal of many a seminary graduate was to teach the laymen what a politically sophisticated Christian ought to know. When the laymen laughed . . . well, they laughed at Jesus, too. When they stopped listening and left the church, they, of course, were reactionary. And when they tried to tell the minister it was possible to be Christian and conservative (or liberal, depending on the minister's politics), it was obvious they just didn't understand.

At a major university in my state there was a sign in front of the university chapel during the presidential election of 1960 which gave the sermon topic for that particular Sunday. It read, "Goldwater or Johnson." The suicide of a young student had just shocked the university community. The students for the most part had enough political sophistication to discern the issues in the election, but most of them had not yet found any meaning to life. The campus was full of students who were broken, empty, afraid, lonely, and guilty, but the sermon, it seemed to me, didn't scratch them where they were itching. And that was sad because they desperately needed to hear something other than political pap. I also tried to make Christianity fit into my political mold, but I found nobody listened because they figured, and quite rightly, that they knew as much about political issues as I did. Only a fool persists in that which does not work.

There have been times when I equated Christianity with an institution. The institution of the church is certainly a place where one would go to find Christianity. However, I have found the institution and Christianity are not the same thing. Suppose I should have an encounter with God so real and so dynamic that I was able to bring others together under my leadership. Suppose further I was able to lead other people into the same experience with God. Soon we would have a full-fledged church institution going (we could call it "The Sons and Daughters of Heavenly Hope"). Now everything would be fine until my children and the children of my followers were old enough to enter the church. Assuming that these young people wanted to enter the church we had formed, they would not necessarily have had the same experience as ours. However, they would see we observed certain rituals, we said prayers in a certain way, we sang certain hymns and we said certain things. It would be only natural that some of these young people should equate all of the ways we did things with the experience we had with God. By the time our grandchildren were old enough to enter the church, the ritual, the prayers, the hymns, and the words would have importance in and of themselves completely apart from any experience with God that we, the original founders of the church, had known.

There was once a man whose job on the railroad was tapping the wheels of the trains. One time someone asked him why he tapped the wheels. His answer, "I don't know why, but I've been doing it for twenty years, and I never miss one." The third generation members of our church could probably say something similar about their reason for being members of the church.

Perhaps something of this sort has happened in the

Christian church. Sometimes the machine no longer produces the same product, but out of respect for the machine we must keep it going. Of course, this isn't universally true in the institution of the church. In every generation there are those who know the experience which is at the heart of the faith. But these are also many more who figure, if they pray, sing, talk, and read the way their forefathers did, they will have the same experience. However, God doesn't have any grandchildren.

I have found that it is especially easy for a minister to equate Christianity with the institution. When you work for a concern, and when you labor to make it a going concern, it is only natural that you tend to overestimate that concern's importance. A lot of ministers (and I include myself) have been so busy getting people into the pews of the church building that we have neglected to get them into the Kingdom of God; sometimes we have been diligent in fattening the church rolls when we should have been diligent in fattening the Book of Life. This is not to say the institution of the church is no longer important. It is, contrary to what a lot of people have to say about it. It is important, not because it is Christianity, but because, when it is faithful, it carries the news that will produce Christianity. It is important because it is a visible sign to the world of something very real and important. But it is a mistake to equate the visible sign with Christianity itself.

There have also been times when I saw a confessional standard as being central to Christianity. I am a minister in a confessional denomination, which is to say my denomination holds to certain confessional statements we believe embody the "givens" of Christianity. It is quite easy to jump from this concept to the belief that Christianity and holding to confessional standards are the same thing. Someone once said the church to which he belonged was split down the middle. One group in the church felt a person ought to be baptized *into* the name of the Father, Son, and Holy Spirit. The other group felt a person ought to be baptized *in* the name of the Father, Son, and Holy Spirit. He said he belonged to one of these groups; he believed deeply in its position, and he would willingly die for that position. "The trouble is," he said, "I can't remember to which group I belong."

What a person believes is important. I have certain convictions about my faith which must stand central in my life; I believe there are those who have weakened the Christian faith by espousing views which are contrary to it. However, when doctrines become more important to me than men; when I am more concerned with a creed than the experience behind the creed; when I see men in terms of my confessional standards rather than in terms of God's love for them, I have missed the point of Christianity.

It is quite possible, it seems to me, for a person to believe every word of every creed in the church, to understand and accept even the minute details of orthodox Christianity, to have a heretic for dinner every evening, and still go to hell. James says, "You believe that God is one; you do well. Even the demons believe—and shudder" (James 2:19). Doctrines, creeds, confessional statements are important and let nothing I have said cause you to think otherwise. But they do not constitute the essence of Christianity.

The question still remains, What then is Christianity?

35

The essence of Christianity is not a moral code, a political philosophy, an institution, nor a confessional statement. Christianity is a relationship—a relationship to Jesus Christ. When a person, be he minister or layman, overlooks this fact, he will find himself involved with something other than the Christian faith. Without that relationship everything is flat and empty. Not too long ago a man came to me and said he was ready to give up on Christianity. "It just doesn't work," he said. "I have tried it, and it just doesn't work." As we talked, it became clear to me this man had not really tried Christianity and found it wanting. His problem was he had never tried real Christianity. He had tried to live by all the rules; he had tried to be involved with the institution (he was an officer in the church); he had tried to believe the creeds, to read the Bible and to say the prayers, but this man had never really understood the necessity of coming into a relationship with Jesus Christ. When he did understand it, it changed his life. Sam Shoemaker knew what he was talking about when he said it was possible to be inoculated so often with the dead germs of Christianity that one becomes immune to the real thing.

When a person becomes a Christian a number of things happen. He is set free from his sin by the atonement of Jesus Christ. As someone has expressed it, "All of your sins are taken and dumped into the ocean, and God has put up a sign that reads *No Fishing.*" One who has encountered Jesus Christ finds himself free to fail. He is no longer working on a production basis but a love basis. Jesus loves him anyway! When a person becomes a Christian, he is given a new joy and meaning in his life. The joy is real and deep, and the meaning is sufficient to

36

make life worthwhile. When a person decides to "take up a cross," he has a place to go and something vitally important to do. More important than anything else, Jesus Christ really, literally, comes to reside in his life.

Every so often when someone is in a difficult situation he says, "I wonder what Jesus would do if He were here." Well, for a Christian the question is not, "What would Jesus do?" but, "What will I do because I am, in a real sense, Jesus."

Paul said, " ... I bow my knees before the Father, from whom every family in heaven and on earth is named, that according to the riches of his glory he may grant you to be strengthened with might through his Spirit in the inner man, and that Christ may dwell in your hearts through faith ... " (Ephesians 3:14–17).

When the Apostle John wanted his readers to know they need have nothing to do with false spirits, he said, "Little children, you are of God, and have overcome them; for he who is in you is greater than he who is in the world" (I John 4:4).

One of the most startling passages in all of the Bible is found in the fifteenth chapter of John. Jesus is talking and He says, "Abide in me and I in you. As the branch cannot bear fruit by itself, unless it abides in the vine, neither can you, unless you abide in me. I am the vine, you are the branches. ... For apart from me you can do nothing" (verses 4–5). That means the power source for the Christian is Jesus. Not only that, it means we can't do anything without being connected to that power source.

Do you know what distinguishing feature I see more than any other in committed Christians? They are worn-out from trying to do the will of God. They have strained

37

so hard to live up to the commandments of God that they have "tired blood." They have never known the freedom about which Jesus spoke. I know a lady for whom the word "sin" is an abstraction. She would be horrified if anyone suggested she was not doing the will of God. She is always at the doors of the church when they are open; she reads her Bible and prays a major portion of each day; she is the first person on hand when someone is in need. Far be it from me to say that sin is good, and, that prayer, Bible reading, and service are evil. They aren't. But the problem with this lady is that she has worked so hard at being a proper Christian, she can no longer smile. She would be the last person to whom I would go if I wanted to introduce someone to a Christian who was alive and radiant.

More ministers are guilty of this kind of Christianity than laymen. Because we are often expected to be better than the "ordinary" Christian, we sometimes work harder at it. Also, because our lives so often don't measure up to what we preach in the pulpit, we feel guilty, and the guilt pushes us harder. Recently my wife and I went to a movie and during the intermission I went back to the concession stand to get some popcorn. As the girl at the counter gave me my change, she asked, "Are you a minister?" I reluctantly admitted to the crime and asked her how she knew. "Oh," she said, "you just look like one." (If you want to destroy a minister's ego, just tell him he looks like a minister.) After I had licked my wounds, I began to think about her observation. Perhaps the girl thought I looked like a minister because I seemed so sad and glum. Perhaps she said to herself, "He looks so miserable and tired, he must be a minister." I hope that wasn't the reason, but if it was, may God forgive me.

When Christians work so hard at their Christianity that it makes them rigid, they have missed one of the major principles of the Christian faith—that to be Christian is to let Jesus do it. The conflict in many Christians' lives comes when Jesus offers to take over their lives. When He offers to enable us to become like Him, when He would transform us into joyful, alive Christians, we say—just like the television commercial—"Please, Jesus, I'd rather do it myself!"

Jesus said, " . . . apart from me you can do nothing" (John 15:5). In other words, Jesus is saying that if we want to be like Him, if we want to be in His will, if we want to be good, pure, righteous, and loving, we must allow Him to make us that way. Christianity is yielding to the Christ in us. The depth of our Christian life and the reality of our Christian life will depend on how much we are willing to allow Jesus to do in our life.

When I was serving a church on Cape Cod, I decided what the church needed was a small group fellowship. And so about fifteen people began to meet together weekly. For the first three meetings I tried to mold the group into my idea of what it ought to be. I did all of the praying and most of the talking. Then one time God told me, "Steve, why don't you shut up and let me do something!" It was hard, but somehow I managed to be quiet and let Jesus Christ take over. From that time on, the small group was one of the most exciting things that happened in my ministry there. I learned a lot from that experience. I learned as long as I am willing to control my own life and the situations in which I find myself, Jesus will let me. But until I am willing to let Jesus do it, nothing will happen.

Once an American was visiting in the home of an English

friend who took him to hear Charles H. Spurgeon preach. As they were leaving the church the Englishman asked his American friend, "Well, what did you think of him?"

"Whom?" the American asked.

"Why, Spurgeon, of course!"

"Oh," replied the American, "to tell you the truth, I was not thinking of Spurgeon. I was thinking of his Christ."

The Christian's constant prayer ought to be a prayer of submission. As the Christian finds obstacles in his life, he ought to turn them over to Jesus Christ admitting he can't overcome them by himself. When a Christian is willing to do that he will find, almost without knowing it, that Jesus is slowly and surely molding the clay into a useful vessel.

Theology is sometimes irrelevant to most people because it is too abstract. The man on the street lives in a world where it is increasingly difficult to be a Christian. He is constantly running and often doesn't understand the race or why he is in it. He is the kind of person who wonders if he can meet the bills at the end of the month and the emptiness at the end of the day. He can't sleep at night because his problems and his sins won't let him. The person for whom Christ died is a woman who is worried about her children and her husband. She doesn't know for sure if she can face another load of wash, another wet diaper, or another hot stove. The people of our world are tired, worried, empty, afraid, lonely, guilty, broken, and hurt. John Doe doesn't care about the historical Jesus. He doesn't want to know about hermeneutical principles, nor does he care about the process of demythologization. It is not important to him that God is the "Ground of Being" or "Ultimate Concern." The men who gather every evening at the neighborhood bar don't know yet that they have "come of age." The person at the bowling alley or the supermarket wants to know, quite simply, what difference Jesus Christ will make in his life. He wants to know if there is a faith which works, and if so, how it works. He wants to find some meaning, if there is meaning. He wants to know God, if there is a God. He wants to be different, if that is possible. That is the reason I would like to look at the nature of the Christ from the perspective of what He has done, and what He is doing for at least one person. There will be no abstractions.

I have experienced the Christ who saves. "Salvation" isn't a popular word these days, but it ought to be. Peter described the experience, "Once you were no people but now you are God's people; once you had not received mercy but now you have received mercy" (I Peter 2:10).

There once was a king who had a son. He loved his son more than all of his lands, riches, and power. But one day the king's son, while playing near the castle, got lost. He was so little, and the world was so big; he couldn't find his way back to the castle. Eventually the little boy ended up in a city of the kingdom, his clothes torn and tattered, begging for bread and fighting for survival.

The king demonstrated his love for his son by turning the kingdom upside down looking for him. A great reward was offered to anyone who could give the king information concerning his whereabouts. The king's armies were pulled back from the battlefield in order to participate in the search. Every avenue of search having been exhausted without success, the king finally resigned himself to the fact that he would probably never see his son again.

Meanwhile, the days blended into years, and the son, having to fend for himself in a cold, uncaring world, forgot about his father, his heritage of kingship, and the early years of his life. He began to run with the wrong crowd and eventually became its leader. He and his band of cutthroats were soon known throughout the kingdom as the most vicious of all criminals. Murder, rape, theft, graft, extortion—nothing was too terrible or too malicious for the young man and his followers. But more than anything else, he hated authority. Whenever the young man would ride past the castle of the king, he would spit on the ground because the king represented authority.

Through a strange set of circumstances, the king learned his lost son had become the kingdom's most wanted criminal. He found out that the son he had loved so deeply, the son for whom he had searched so long had turned against everything for which the king had lived his life. And now, the king was faced with a terrible dilemma. The kingdom had its laws, and it was mandatory that those laws be obeyed. However, the king loved his son and could not bear the thought of him going before an executioner. But the king was left with no choice and, on the following day, the son was arrested, brought before a judge and condemned to die.

On the night before the day of execution, the old king made his way to the cell in which the son waited. The lines on the old man's face were deep, his walk was slow, tears streamed down his face, and his voice trembled with emotion as he spoke, "My son," he said, "I have loved you with a great love, but you became lost and I could not find you. And now it has all come to this. Tomorrow you must die." There was a long pause before the old man spoke again. When he did speak, his voice was quiet and pleading. "My son," he continued, "I have decided you will not have to die. I have decided you will have your freedom. It is my hope your freedom will bring you home, but, be that as it may, you are free."

There was a cynical smile on the young man's face as he walked away from the kingdom's prison. "That stupid old man." he said, "He thinks that I will return to the castle. Well, he is more senile than I thought."

It was weeks later when the young man discovered the price which had been paid for his freedom. He found out that on the day he was to die, his father-king had taken his place on the chopping block. The father had paid a terrible price for his son's freedom—he had given his life.

You wonder how the story ended? Do you want to know what happened to the son, whether or not he returned to the castle and fulfilled his father's dream? To be honest, I don't know exactly how that story ends because it is your story, and it is my story. We write the conclusion. You see, I am like that son. I, too, have rebelled against my Father-God. I was angry, hateful, bitter, cynical, and revengeful, but my Father loved me anyway. He loved me so much He would come to me and plead with me and die on a cross for me. The acceptance of that fact has become a central theme of my life. I have been declared free from my sin, even though I am a sinner. I have been given fellowship with Christ, even though I don't deserve it. I have experienced the Christ who saves.

I have also experienced the Christ who loves. One of the greatest discoveries of my life was the discovery that God really loves me. It isn't a pious platitude or a worn-out slogan either. Its proof is there for all men to see! God, spread-eagled on crossbeams, between two crooks, on the town garbage heap, dying in my place.

We live in a world which places its inhabitants on a production basis. If you produce, you will be successful, honored, accepted, and loved. If you don't, you won't. It is quite easy to transfer this attitude into the realm of one's relationship to God. A lot of people see God as sitting in the heavens waiting to zap anyone who gets out of line. But the more I know of Jesus the more I realize he loved me, period, and not because. When my relationship with Christ was established, it became a relationship based on His love, His faithfulness, His action—not mine. Sometimes I don't love Him at all. There are many times when I want to forget about the whole commitment and become a pagan. There are times when I break every promise I have ever made to Him. But the relationship doesn't depend on what I do or what I don't do. It is dependent on what he does. His love is not conditional; it has no strings attached; it is pure and single-minded. Were His love anything else, I would never have experienced it. In my relationship with Christ, I have also experienced care and understanding. It's like the story of a little boy who lived in an orphanage. One day each child received a basket of fruit from a generous donor. All the children, with the exception of the one lad, ate their fruit. Instead he put his basket of fruit in the dormitory window above his bed. When someone asked him why he had not eaten his fruit, he said, "I wanted people to see that someone cares for me." That child's need is reflected in the lives of adults, too.

A woman who had been through a terrible tragedy in her life told me recently, "Steve, if I only knew that someone cared, all of this would be bearable."

One of the great facts about human existence is man's need to have someone care and understand. More often than not, when people hope to have that need filled by other people, they are disappointed. For instance, the care and understanding which is given by parents to their children is often mixed with self-interest. Many times the parental desire for children to be good, to be successful, to make something of themselves can be translated, "Don't make your parents ashamed. Let us be proud of you in front of our friends. Let no one think we have raised you improperly." The care and understanding we receive from friends is also not as pure as we would like to think. Sometimes friendships are built on an I'll-scratch-your-back-if-you-scratch-mine basis.

Shakespeare, in *The Tragedy of Julius Caesar,* has Cassius say, "A friend should bear his friend's infirmities, but Brutus makes mine greater than they are." The experience of Cassius, who was himself self-centered, can be found in the experience of almost everyone. One of the most difficult lessons life teaches us about ourselves and about others is that there is very little care and understanding completely pure and free of self-interest. This is not to say there is no care and understanding in the world. It is, however, to say a person who expects completely pure motives in himself and in others is in for a lot of disappointment.

45

The one place where we can find One who cares completely, where we can find One who understands completely is in the person of Jesus Christ. Hardly a day passes that someone doesn't speak to me about an experience of God's care and His understanding in particular situations. A woman whose husband had been out of work for months and whose children, during those long months, were deprived of necessities, told me, "Pastor, God has been good. Without Him we could not have made it." An alcoholic said, "Steve, when I realized how much God cared for me in Christ, it made all the difference in the world." A college student said he didn't think anyone could understand the pressures of his life until he met Jesus Christ. I would add my testimony to theirs. Sometimes, when I think my ministry isn't worth the effort, and it makes little difference to anyone whether or not I remain, I remember that Jesus knows my name, and if He knows my name then I can trust Him. I remember that, and I am glad.

I have also experienced the Christ who leads and sustains. One of the great lessons I have learned from Him is that no accidents happen to Christians. After college my wife and I, acting on what we thought to be the leading of Christ, came to Boston for seminary. After being in seminary for only a month, we found we were going to have a baby. I was working as a production manager for a Boston radio station and doing a morning show. I would get up at 3:30 A.M. every morning and go to the station. I was off the air at nine o'clock and then rode the subway to school where I remained in class until around two or three in the afternoon. Then I would head back to the station for my production work, often not finishing until eight or nine in the evening. After work I would "hit the books" until midnight, then up again at 3:30 A.M. in order to go through the same grind. Now that is no schedule for an ambitious energetic man, much less for a lazy one. I am of the latter breed.

My wife went to spend a few days with relatives, and I walked the beaches in and around Boston for the greater part of two weeks. I asked God why, if He wanted me in the ministry, He had let me get into this kind of situation. I told God how angry and hurt I was. I shouted at Him and begged Him and came near cursing Him, but there was no answer. And so, I dropped out of seminary, finally facing the fact that bills had to be paid. I wanted more than anything in the world to become a minister, but now it seemed impossible. I had very little hope of ever returning to seminary.

When my wife came home, we turned the situation over to Christ, trusting Him to do what was best. We moved into an apartment in the suburbs and for a year settled down to the life of lay people. Now that I look back on that year, I can see it was one of the most valuable and important of my life. My wife and I learned things we never would have discovered in a hundred years of seminary. The next summer Christ led us to a small church that needed a pastor. I was able to return to seminary and also pay the bills. The principle? Jesus Christ knows what He is doing even when the Christian doesn't. When we turn our lives over to Christ, we can trust Him. My wife and I had given our lives to Christ, but we couldn't see how He was working until we looked back.

Finally, I have experienced the Christ who serves. Matthew wrote, " . . . whoever would be great among you must be your servant, and whoever would be first among you must be your slave; even as the Son of man came not to be served but to serve, and to give his life as a ransom for many" (Matthew 20:26–28). As my relationship with Christ has deepened, I have found that He is a servant to me. His servanthood manifests itself in the fact that there is nothing I can do for Him. He doesn't need my money, my time, my love, my help, my work, my life. He is a servant, also, because He is always closer than I know, ready to meet all of my needs if I will only allow Him.

If all of the above seems self-centered to you, you are right. However, this must always be the starting point for any relationship with Christ. He is always the initiator in everything. He is the servant who has come to us first. The spiritual principle is this—you can't meet the needs of other people until your needs have been met. Love comes when we have first been loved. We are able to understand and care for others only when we have become secure in the care and understanding of Christ. We don't become the sustaining factor in the life of another person until we allow Christ to become the sustaining factor in our own lives. We can't really be a servant until we allow Jesus to be a servant to us. The zeal with which many people set out to change the world dies quickly because this principle is overlooked. Churches often are ready to throw in the towel before they get started in their mission because they have not allowed Jesus Christ to meet their needs before trying themselves to meet the needs of the world. Without the prior and continuing relationship between the believer and his Lord, the church will die, the world will be deprived of a necessary witness, the task will go unfinished, and the future will be empty.

3

THE CHURCH

Husbands, love your wives, as Christ loved the church and gave himself up for her, that he might sanctify her, having cleansed her by the washing of water with the word, that he might present the church to himself in splendor, without spot or wrinkle or any such thing, that she might be holy and without blemish.

EPHESIANS 5:25–27

And I tell you, you are Peter and on this rock I will build my church, and the powers of death shall not prevail against it.

MATTHEW 16:18

WE LIVE IN AN AGE OF CRITICISM and one of the most popular objects of that criticism has been the church. With obviously more glee than sadness, the multitude of critics line up to throw their relevant rocks and insightful invectives at the church. Throughout the church the laymen rest uncomfortably on the comfortable pews, and one can notice the sounds of guilt mingled with the noise of solemn assemblies. From every corner of the church, laments can be heard about the post-Christian era and the death of God. They say acute ecclesiastical senility has set in, and it will only be a matter of time before a eulogy will be read.

They say the church will die when its old folks die. Meanwhile, many members of the old dying institution either join the ranks of the rock throwers or wring their hands and whine.

Before someone shovels a pile of dirt and plants a monument, I wonder if it would be possible for a young man who loves the church to offer a suggestion. Check the coffin before you cover up the grave. There just may not be a corpse. It would not be the first time somebody planned a funeral for the church and found the main attraction had a previous engagement. A man by the name of Saul tried to hold the church's funeral even before it was out of its infancy. The arrangements weren't wasted though. They were used to bury the old man in Saul who was then reborn into Paul, the apostle, the missionary, the church leader, the New Testament writer. Then in A.D. 64 a man by the name of Nero prepared the church's funeral. Julian in A.D. 368 said he would embalm the cadaver, dig the grave and bury the church. A hundred years ago Friedrich Nietzsche said the church's funeral would take place before the dawn of the twentieth century. Nero, Julian and Nietzsche have gone the way of all flesh having been survived by the church they tried so terribly hard to bury. Considering past experiences I would suggest that somebody check the coffin before you cover up the grave. There may be a surprise.

I would like to offer a few observations from one who didn't figure on working for a dead organization. First, if the church dies of anything, it will be from the endless jabber of ecclesiastical nit-pickers who feel guilty if they don't feel guilty, and from the babble of dreamworld thinkers who would rather have their pet political philosophy incorporated into the latest resolution than to see men confronted with the reality of Jesus Christ. Some people believe that cynicism plus education equals a prophet. That isn't true. This is, cynicism plus education equals an educated cynic. The educated cynics are usually harmless unless others are conned into believing they are prophets. When that happens, and people start listening, the resultant ecclesiastical guilt complex makes anything that Freud blamed on the church insignificant by comparison. I didn't consider the church was perfect when I joined it. (Had it been, it would never have accepted me). But I did see there were people in the church who, despite their failings and the church's imperfections, had found something real and meaningful. If those people had invited me to a seminar on the outdated church, I would never have joined. Thank God they took me to Jesus instead. If the church dies, it will be because we heard so many false prophets that when the real thing came along we didn't recognize it.

Second, Jesus said all of the "powers of death" would not prevail against His church. I'll accept that! To be perfectly honest, if I thought the church was composed of only its human members I would agree with the nitpickers. But there is another factor most people outside the church overlook. There is the presence of God. That presence is supernatural, and it is sovereign. If you happen to be the type of person who can't accept the supernatural, if you believe the sovereignity of God is only a relic from an outdated creed, then I don't blame you for trying to bring in the Kingdom with your panicked manipulations. I would, too! If, however, you haven't placed the nails in God's coffin yet, you will have another view. You will believe, no matter how slowly or painfully, Jesus Christ is working within His church that "He might present the church to Himself in splendor, without spot or wrinkle or any such thing, that she might be holy and without blemish" (Ephesians 5:27). Believing that, you will be free to carry on the work of the church trusting Him eventually to work His will.

Third, for a patient who is supposed to be on her death bed, the church has an uncanny ability to kick. It is the church that gave birth to the civil rights movement and the war on poverty. It is the church, through such movements as Campus Crusade for Christ and Inter-Varsity Christian Fellowship that is being felt on the college campus long after the cynics have sold out. In the ghetto of New York, you will find a Young Life staff worker; by the bedside of a "mainliner" who is trying to kick the habit, you will find Teen Challenge; in the stadiums and auditoriums of the world, you will find thousands gathered to hear the Gospel preached by Billy Graham; in the heat of the city on a summer night, you will find Pocket Testament League giving men the good news of Jesus Christ—that is the church. Around the world, missionaries are telling the story of Jesus with words and acts of mercy; at the Koinonia Farm of Americus, in the state of Georgia, men labor to illustrate the relevance of Jesus Christ to rural realities; in Christian Business Men's Committee, business men are being confronted with the person of Christ; Christian Business and Professional Women and Christian Women's Clubs are reaching women with the Gospel. If all this, and much, much more, is the last gasp of a dying church then more organizations ought to die. It would be good for them.

Fourth, although God may have given up on much of the ecclesiastical structure and hierarchy, He may not be finished with His laymen. Most Protestants believe in the priesthood of all believers. That means, among other things, that each Christian is a minister in his own right. It means the layman's view is not inferior to that of his pastor. It means that most Protestants see the terrible dangers in a clergy-dominated hierarchy. However, it is one thing to say you believe these things and quite another to act on them. For instance, when a minister talks about how the laymen in his church ought to become active ministers themselves and then is shocked when the laymen turn in directions he feels are improper, the minister doesn't really want the laymen involved (except as boy ministers following in the footsteps of their more educated, sophisticated, theologically relevant senior minister). When the hierarchy of any denomination speaks to political issues in such a way as to ignore the view of many of their constituents, and in such a way as to imply that any other view is less than Christian, then the hierarchy really doesn't want lay involvement.

We live in a time of major social change. The upheaval both within the church and outside the church is catastrophic. During the recent years of change and upheaval, the laymen in the church have looked to their clergy and theologians to give direction and meaning. Instead of direction and meaning, they have been told all too often that everything they have held to be important and true is no longer relevant. They have been told all too often about a dead God (or at most a sick one) and a religionless Christianity. Many laymen have felt, and justifiably so, that if the leaders who ought to know could no longer believe the faith was relevant, who were they to argue—and so they left the church.

Other laymen have decided to check for themselves and as a result of their endeavors have found faith is not only relevant, but is the most exciting thing they have ever discovered. Lay Witness Missions, where laymen tell other laymen about their exciting discoveries, are spreading throughout the church. If I were a betting man, I would put a lot of money on these laymen. They just may be God's instrument for renewal.

No, I don't believe the church is going to die. It will sometimes be sick, hurt, lazy, and afraid, but it won't die. There are too many people who love the church. They won't let her die. God has too much at stake in the church. He won't let her die. To repeat, check the coffin, there just may not be a corpse.

Nothing I have said so far should be taken to mean that I believe the church is beyond criticism. In fact, I believe criticism is vital to the life of the church. My quarrel is with the type of criticism. There must be some criteria by which one can judge the validity of the criticism. Some suggestions follow.

I believe *a critic of the church must be a part of the church.* I say this for two reasons. Many of the major tenets of the Christian faith are by their nature quite subjective. Of course Christianity is a religion which affirms the belief that God has acted in history. However, those historical acts are worthless unless there follows experience. Regeneration, justification, sanctification, repentance, forgiveness, salvation are more than ecclesiastical catchwords. They are words which describe the experiences of the Christian. The man, who has never experienced these things and who has never become thereby a member of the Body of Christ, can certainly speak truth about the church, but in the final analysis his criticism is not valid because he has applied his criticism without thoroughly understanding his subject. Once there was a college professor who was a bachelor and whose favorite lecture was "Ten Commandments for Parents." After a number of years of giving this lecture, the bachelor professor got married and was blessed with his first child. He changed the topic of his lecture to "Ten Suggestions for Parents." Later, his second child was born, and once again he changed the title to "Some Thoughts on Parenthood." After his third child was born he gave up lecturing. The principle is this: criticism is easy and often wrong when a non-Christian directs it toward something as subjective as Christianity.

Another reason a critic should be a part of the church to which he directs his criticism is a matter of trust. When Karl Marx criticised the church, it was because he saw the church as standing in his way. His criticism at times was perhaps true, but his motives were not the motives of the church nor were his goals the goals of the church. His criticism, in order to be used by the church, must be interpreted and applied by a member of the church who sees truth in that criticism in terms of the purposes of the church. To criticize the Society for the Prevention of Cruelty to Children because it did not protect Mrs. Murphy's cat may be valid as an observation, but it is not valid criticism. One would be quite justified in suspecting that the critic has a special interest in Mrs. Murphy's cat and not in the work of the Society for the Prevention of Cruelty to Children.

Another criterion one could use to measure the validity of a critic is to *see if he has anything other than criticism.* Only a fool would be so stupid as to see nothing deserving of praise in the church. Just a cursory glance at the church's great humanitarian efforts, its contribution to scholarship, its efforts at reconciliation, would be enough to cause at least a modicum of praise. When a critic sees only one side of the ecclesiastical coin, others should question his motives and his objectivity.

I have an aquaintance who hates the Christian Church. I have never, in all of the years I have known him, heard him speak one word of praise for it. I have seen others, caught up in his passionate denunciations of the church, joining with him in his tirade against it. But if they had taken the time to check, they would have found this man was at one time turned away from the church in a time of need. The fact that it happened ought to give all of us in the church pause. However, one cannot indict the whole church for the sin of one church or one individual anymore than one can indict the whole food industry because one loaf of bread was stale.

A valid critic ought to be able to offer viable alternatives and solutions to the problems he sees. It is so easy to criticize. In a homiletics class in seminary I remember one student who was critical of another student because in the pulpit his glasses reflected a light that hung from the ceiling of the chapel. The solution to the problem would be for the student to remove his glasses (and thus be unable to see his notes and the congregation) or to have someone remove the light from the ceiling (and thus be faced with the wrath of the dean). Because neither the solution nor alternative was acceptable, the criticism was not valid.

The next time someone tells you the church is irrelevant, ask him how he proposes to make it more relevant and when he proposes to start. When someone tells you there ought to be more lay involvement, ask him to describe his program. The next time someone tells you the church is dying, ask him what he proposes to do to make it live. One of the difficulties I had with trying to put into practice those things I learned in seminary was feasibility. They all looked great on paper. They sounded good, but many of them just didn't work. I have learned to take the criticism of those who have no viable program with a grain of salt.

A critic must be called by God to criticize. A man doesn't become a prophet because he wants to be a prophet, or because others say he is a prophet, or because prophets are in short supply. A man is called by God to become a prophet. Amos, perhaps the most angry critic in the Bible, was called to be a prophet. Read again his dialogue with Amaziah:

"And Amaziah said to Amos, 'O seer, go, flee away to the land of Judah, and eat bread there, and prophesy there; but never again prophesy at Bethel, . . . for it is a temple of the kingdom.'

"Then Amos answered Amaziah, 'I am no prophet, nor a prophet's son [refering to the false prophets with which Amaziah and the people were familiar]; but I am a herdsman, and a dresser of sycamore trees, and the Lord took me from following the flock, and the Lord said to me, "Go prophesy to my people Israel"'" (Amos 7:12–15).

There are too many people who, not having been called

by God, try to assume the mantle of a prophet. Had they waited until God called them their criticism would not have been so superficial and naive, for they would have been speaking God's words and not their own.

I am tired of cynics who call themselves realists, of those who feel the essence of sophistication lies in negativism. I am tired of blasé people, espousing blasé ideas and calling it intelligent Christianity. I am tired of people who aren't happy unless they can stand around, wring their hands and spout cliché criticisms of the church. I am not so foolish as to think what I have to say will cause a change, but I do feel better for having said it.

The church does need renewal, and one would have to be blind to deny it. Throughout the church one can see theological and institutional uncertainty. Throughout the church everybody is talking about "mission" but very few know what mission is. Ten years ago the leaders of the church admitted there were problems. During that period most leaders spoke of the need for drastic changes in the institution. However, the difference between then and now is one of confidence. During the fifties and early sixties most ecclesiastical leaders felt, given the proper techniques, programs, and leadership, the problems would be solved. Today we are not nearly so confident. Ministers and denominational leaders admit quite frankly they don't have the answers. They see the church in a decline both statistically and spiritually; they hear laymen talk about how disillusioned they are with the faith; they see most people outside the church are indifferent to the church; they feel uncertain about the

59

message of the church; they see theological absolutes disappearing and institutional structures crumbling. The feeling of many people who lead and love the church is one of overwhelming helplessness.

Helplessness is not a virtue if you are an airline pilot or an engineer, but it should be considered a blessing when you find it in a church which has lost its way. I say this because of a spiritual fact which lies at the very base of Christianity. Most of us have heard since we were children that God helps those who help themselves, a cliché which teaches only a part of the truth. Sometimes God does help those who help themselves, and sometimes He doesn't. But I'll tell you something that is almost always true within the realm of the Christian faith: God helps those who *can't* help themselves—*and who know it*. The Bible talks about a God who knew the helplessness of mankind, a God who searched and found man because man wasn't capable of searching for and finding God. The central theme of the Bible is a theme of love for the unlovely, strength for the weak, home for the homeless, understanding for the misunderstood, salvation for the broken, help for the helpless. The words of Jacob are the words of every Christian, "I am not worthy of the least of all the steadfast love and all the faithfulness which thou hast shown to thy servant ... " (Genesis 32:10).

I consider this then as axiomatic to the Christian Church: If renewal comes it will not come from the efforts of man; if renewal comes it will come from the efforts of God directing the efforts of men. If the church would once again become a prime mover among men, it will not be because the church used the proper techniques, instituted the proper programs, and enlisted the proper leadership. It will be because the church makes a declaration of spiritual and institutional bankruptcy and once again turns to its source which is God. The prophet Jeremiah put it this way, "For I know the plans I have for you, says the Lord, plans for welfare and not for evil, to give you a future and a hope. Then you will call upon me and come and pray to me, and I will hear you. You will seek me and find me; when you seek me with all your heart ... " (Jeremiah 29:11–13).

When the church finds it has lost its way, that its efforts are futile, its programs useless and its leaders are frightened, it is time for a season of prayer—not the short invocation, or the perfunctory "Hi, God" prayer, but real, deep, searching prayer. I recently attended a meeting which was designed to plan the future of my denomination in my area. Nobody, including myself, suggested we begin with prayer. And so this committee met and planned without so much as a nod in the direction of God. How ludicrous! What audacity it took for us to make plans for the future of God's Church without consulting God!

I don't believe genuine renewal will come to the church until men who know how to organize, raise money, preach, and administrate also learn how to pray. I don't believe the church will be renewed until we, the people of the church, realize all of the power that is needful resides in God. When the church starts to put prayer before programs, and a communion with God before committees to study God, there will be a fire started in the church which all the forces of hell will not be able to put out.

We in the church have been trying to produce a lot of

61

things artificially when we should have been on our knees praying for the real thing. For instance, take motivation. Every year enough literature comes across my desk to give a garbage collector a nervous breakdown. Almost all of it is designed to motivate me or to teach me to motivate the members of my church. If I use a new stewardship program, I am told, I will be able to vastly increase the total giving in the church. If I will only form some study groups and use the enclosed material, they say, I will find that finally the people of the church will get involved with the many social problems of our time. They say that a new church school curriculum will produce Christians who care. They tell me there is an exciting new way to get teen-agers involved in the program of the church. If I am frustrated with the ministry I am invited to attend the pastor's school where I will receive fresh insight and renewed vigor. It is all a part of the process of artificial stimulation.

The Apostle Paul didn't need that kind of motivation. He said, "Of this gospel I was made a minister according to the gift of God's grace which was given me by the working of his power. To me, though I am the very least of all the saints, this grace was given, to preach to the Gentiles the unsearchable riches of Christ ... " (Ephesians 3:7–8). Paul didn't go to a conference to find motivation, nor did he become involved in a program; he went to God.

It is no accident that one of the symbols for the Holy Spirit is fire. If we want to get somebody moving, we say we would like to build a fire under them. Someone once asked John Wesley why so many people came to hear him preach. "Get on fire for God," he said, "and men will come to see you burn!" The Holy Spirit, the reality of God in us, is not theological verbiage. The Holy Spirit is a Person who constantly stirs up, excites, prods, and motivates us. One time I heard Gordon Cosby say the church will never be motivated outward until it takes a journey inward. Elizabeth O'Connor, who is the chronicler of the Church of the Saviour in Washington, D.C. (where Gordon Cosby is pastor), elaborates, "This God with whom we will be engaged for the rest of our days comes to us across a great distance, and at the same time He is the divine force at the core of our own lives. ... As people on an inward-outward journey, we are committed to taking whatever time is needed to develop an interior life—a life of prayer. ... We will take the time to be with God in the quiet places of our spirit, so that we can come to know a different quality of life." The tongues of fire that rested on the apostles of Jesus at Pentecost weren't given by a homiletics professor nor by an artist in a denominational public relations department. The tongues of fire came from God. Renewal will come when the church is motivated. Real motivation comes only from God.

Direction is also necessary for renewal. Direction must also come from God. One time after Jesus had given a teaching that was particularly repugnant to the Pharisees, the disciples of Jesus went to Him and told Him how the Pharisees felt. Jesus answered, "Every plant which my heavenly Father has not planted will be rooted up. Let them alone; they are blind guides. And if a blind man leads a blind man, both will fall into a pit" (Matthew 15:13–14). I wonder what Jesus would say about the ministers and leaders in the twentieth-century church. Perhaps He would see how we set our goals with the headlines, and how we gauge our plans from expediency and would say that we are blind guides, too.

I am convinced the reason the church has often been in the wrong place, at the wrong time, with the wrong message has been our inability to listen when God was speaking. I believe many of the urban problems we now face would have been well on the way to solution had the church listened when, ten years ago, God told us to stay and minister in the city. I believe the racial tensions of our time would never have reached the frightening stage where they are today had the church listened when God told us about love and care and involvement. I believe war would have been banished if the church had listened when God told us to evangelize. God has a plan for His church, but, if we don't listen to Him when He would reveal that plan, we will continue to run in endless circles rejoicing in the fact that at least we are moving.

One of the most exciting things about the Book of Acts is the way the church moved only at the direction of God. At Pentecost the disciples didn't know about the future. They didn't know where God would lead, and so they waited. Luke tells us when Peter spoke before the Council, he was first "filled with the Holy Spirit." He was led. After Paul was converted on the road to Damascus, Jesus told him, " ... but rise and enter the city, and you will be told what you are to do" (Acts 9:6) Peter's decision to visit the home of Cornelius was not a decision which was based on the need of the Gentiles to hear the Gospel. He was specifically sent there by God. Paul and Silas were forbidden by the Holy Spirit to speak a word in Asia. And then they tried to go to Bithynia, "but the Spirit of Jesus did not allow them" (Acts 16:7). Paul went to Macedonia not out of ambition or even out of compassion. He went to Macedonia because God led him there. Over and over again Luke tells us about the people of the early church who were strong and successful in their mission because they were obedient to a God who had plans for them.

God still has plans for His church. Our problem is one of allowing Him to reveal those plans. If for every minute of planning for the future and the present of the church, we spent a minute of praying for God to lead, the results would be astounding. David C. Searfoss, the minister of St. Paul's Eastern United Church in Ottawa, Ontario, saw those astounding results in his church. It began at a renewal conference when a number of individuals decided God wasn't as dead as they had thought. Small groups began to meet together for prayer and fellowship. He writes, "We ask God to show us what mission He has for us individually, as groups, and as a church. As a downtown church, we are surrounded by problems: low-income people, school dropouts, delinquents, the purposeless—all those unreached and unreachable by the usual ecclesiastical program. There are many Protestant students at a university just blocks away from us, and most of these students don't even know we exist. No one knows how many lonely, single people there are living in rooming houses in our neighborhood. In our groups we're starting to listen for marching orders." *Groups That Work* includes this further statement: " ... We're sure that we'll always need to be 'with Him.' But we are equally sure that as we get to know Him better, we will

65

hear the command to go again and again." God is a God who directs when we are willing to ask and listen. If He doesn't then we are wasting our time, for experience has proven that most of us don't know what we are doing.

The power that is necessary to make the motivation and the direction worth the effort also must come from God. When one pauses to consider the forces over which the church must prevail if it is to survive, it is frightening. There is a new, lusty, materialistic, powerful, and hostile paganism afoot that could reduce the church to ashes were it not sustained by a power beyond itself. A lot of people in the church don't recognize this fact and therefore continue to put their hope in the same power that sustains the paganism. For instance, the power of the world depends, among other things, on the ability to manipulate, to coerce, and to control. When the church tries to match the world's ability to manipulate, coerce, and control, it will fail. First, it will fail because of sheer weakness. When the church tries to manipulate (e.g. in legislation, governmental programs, foreign policy), the response of the world is laughter. Having spent a number of years in commercial broadcasting, I have watched the reaction of the news media to the numerous resolutions of ecclesiastical councils. That reaction is often a mixture of incredulity and condescending tolerance. The comment of an elephant to a flea climbing the elephant's leg with the intent of murder is, "Oh, really." The church's position is analogous to that of the flea.

Second, the church will fail when it uses the power that is used by the world because the church is playing in a different game. Paul describes the game we ought to be playing this way, "For though we live in the world we are not carrying on a worldly war, for the weapons of our warfare are not worldly but have divine power to destroy strongholds. We destroy arguments and every proud obstacle to the knowledge of God, and take every thought captive to obey Christ ... " (II Corinthians 10:3-5). The game in which the church ought to play is the game of bringing all men to the "knowledge of God" and of bringing the thoughts of all men under captivity to Christ. This is not to say Christians should not be involved in concerns other than these. They should! In fact, an individual Christian who is not involved in the political movements of his society, who is not involved in the foreign policy of his country, who is not involved in the legislation of his congress is not fulfilling his obligation as a Christian. However, the church ought to be extremely careful when it, as a body, enters these waters lest it lose the game in which it is primarily involved.

The power of the church that comes from God is different from the power of the world. It is, first, a power that unifies. The ecumenical movement has much to commend it. However, when the ecumenical movement draws its momentum from expedience (i.e. fall in membership, lack of funds, etc.), when its goal is the power that comes from bigness, when its end is "as many people as possible believing as little as possible," it will fail. That failure will come not because those involved were insincere or uncommitted or irrelevant. Failure will come because those involved didn't realize true unity is spiritual, not structural. The power that will finally unite Christians comes from God. When Christians are drawn to the cross, they are drawn to each other. When we try to move toward each other while forgetting about Him, we will be wasting time.

The power God offers His church is also a power that convicts and converts. So often we in the church have tried to bring souls into the Kingdom "kicking and screaming." God doesn't work that way. If we are dependent on Him, He will prepare men for the reception of Jesus Christ in their lives. We make a terrible mistake when, instead of depending on this power, we revamp our message and repackage our Lord hoping the pill will be easier for Joe Pagan to swallow. I am convinced the reason so many people don't listen and don't want to listen to the Gospel is not because of the inferior packaging, but because of inferior power. When Philip was directed by the Holy Spirit to the Ethiopian eunuch, Philip didn't have to convince him of his need for a Saviour because the Ethiopian had already been prepared. When Philip got to him he was reading the fifty-third chapter of Isaiah, and all Philip had to do was to explain its meaning. When the Ethiopian was finally baptized Philip could not take the credit because he had only been an instrument wielded by the power of God (Acts 8:26–39).

When nobody listens to the Gospel, it is because the church isn't listening to God. Everyone talks about awakening, revival, and renewal, but it won't come until we depend on the power of God to convict and convert. We are required to be faithful witnesses, to make introductions, to speak of what we have seen and heard. God must do the rest because, quite simply, we can't. Anyone who has ever tried to "engineer" a revival knows it.

The power of God also produces compassion. One of the reasons a lot of people in the church (and outside the church, too) are turned off by the problems of the city, the cries of the hungry, and the ravages of war isn't because they haven't been told. They have—over and over again. The problem is that human beings aren't by nature compassionate. Tell a man who has no motive other than profit and guilt that he must get involved in the problems of the city, and he will either ask you how much money he can make at it, or he will become involved because he feels guilty. Actions based on profit die when the money stops; actions based on guilt die when enough has been done to ease the rationalized conscience. But, if you take a man to Jesus, compassion comes naturally because it is the compassion of Jesus in the man's life. It is no accident that after every major spiritual awakening in the history of the church there has followed a great outpouring of compassion for the hurt, the lonely, the bound, the hungry, and the tired. That is just naturally what happens when a person gets next to God for any length of time at all.

Finally, the power God would give His church is a power that sustains. The reason so many flaming reformers go out to change the world and then quit before they get started is that they have no sustaining power. They begin with plenty of enthusiasm; they have mastered the methods of social reformation; they are committed to the reformation; they are sure of their goals, but they die when the obstacles appear. This should never be true of the church because there is a reservoir of supernatural power available which will sustain us if we will only use it.

It was the sustaining power of God that enabled the church to survive the persecutions of Nero and Julian. During the Dark Ages, it was the church that provided the thread of continuity for civilization because it was the only institution which possessed sustaining power. During the fourteenth and fifteenth centuries, Christianity survived political changes which almost destroyed it in Asia and Europe. It survived because the Reformation, and later the Counter-Reformation, became the instrument of God's sustaining power. Across the pages of history march such giants as Luther, Latimer, Zwingli, Calvin, Melanchthon, Cranmer, Knox, Wesley, Carey, Whitfield, Moody, Bonhoeffer. These men stayed when others would not or could not. They stayed because they had a power source that didn't dry up when the going got difficult.

A man who had given his life serving in the slums of London was asked why he did not give it all up and run away. He answered, "Because a strange man on a cross won't let me." If the church is faithful, it will still be around praying, working, loving, caring, understanding, reconciling long after other organizations and other men have given up. Why? Because the church has roots in a God who sustains by His power.

I am a young minister in the church of Christ. From that vantage point I can see a lot of problems in the church, but beyond the problems I can see a God who "loved the church and gave himself up for her." Because I can see Him, I am glad I am young, and I am glad I am a minister in His church.

4

THE WORLD

For God so loved the world that he gave his only Son, that whoever believes in him should not perish but have eternal life.

JOHN 3:16

In the world you have tribulation; but be of good cheer, I have overcome the world.

JOHN 16:33

Do not be conformed to this world but be transformed by the renewal of your mind, that you may prove what is the will of God, what is good and acceptable and perfect.

ROMANS 12:2

IT'S LATE in the afternoon, and a young man is walking across the Boston University Bridge. As he walks alone, no one speaks to him, no one smiles at him, no one even nods a greeting his way. The young man is a foreign student at the Massachusetts Institute of Technology. He has come to America to study and learn so that when he returns to the place of his birth he will make a meaningful contribution. As he walks alone on the bridge, the workmen are putting up signs in the city befitting the coming religious holiday. The signs bid the people to celebrate the holiday with a new pair of shoes, some guns and cannons with which to play war, and a bottle of Four Roses.

The young man walks alone down Commonwealth Avenue, past the university student union building and the School of Theology where he turns left and walks under the archway of the university chapel with its cross on the altar. He pauses in front of the law and education building, looking up at its seventeen stories of height. On his face there is perplexity, in his eyes there is loneliness and his hand trembles slightly as he reaches for the door at the main entrance. He walks from there to the elevator and presses the lighted button for the seventeenth floor. Getting off on that floor, the young man quickly walks to a window, opens it and jumps to his death.

Albert Camus, the late French philosopher and Nobel Prize winner, has said the only question with which modern man must deal is the question of whether or not he should commit suicide. He said further that if a man decides to commit suicide there is nothing else to say, but if he decides to live he must find reasons for living. I believe Camus perceived the true nature of the world. Take away the rose-colored glasses and the pills, and the world is a pretty terrifying place. Among the alternative reactions, one of the most attractive is suicide. (One does not necessarily commit suicide with sleeping pills. It is often less painful with eight hours of work, eight hours of sleep, eight hours of television and a six-pack of beer.)

A college friend of mine once told me his life was utterly empty. He said he hoped to find something in his studies in philosophy to fill the emptiness. When I first entered the ministry a man came into my study, told me his story and said he was thinking of suicide. I could see his point! A man with whom I once worked in broadcasting had money, friends, and position. He told me, "Steve, sometimes at night when I am alone, I cry." A woman with whom I am acquainted said her life was so miserable she could no longer hide it from her friends. And a beautiful, young Hollywood movie star took her own life. Her reason? She was lonely. The only question with which modern man must deal is the question of whether or not he should commit suicide.

Matthew Arnold, whose perception of the world surpassed that of most men, said it well in "Rugby Chapel."

> What is the course of the life
> Of mortal men on the earth?
> Most men eddy about
> Here and there—eat and drink,
> Chatter and love and hate,
> Gather and squander, are raised
> Aloft, are hurled in the dust,
> Striving blindly, achieving
> Nothing; and then they die—
> Perish;—and no one asks
> Who or what they have been,
> More than he asks what waves,
> In the moonlit solitudes mild
> Of the midmost ocean, have swelled,
> Foamed for a moment, and gone.

As I dimly perceive the darkness of my world, I say to myself, "The only way to find meaning and peace in this world and to gain a world to come is give myself a quality of goodness." And so I make an effort at goodness. I try to love the lady down the street who is always complaining about my dog. I try to control my temper and my tongue. I visit those who are sick and lonely. I make an honest effort to rid myself of pride, lust, and bitterness. But at night when I take off my smiling face for the evening, when I am alone, when I don't have to pretend anymore, when I have to be honest, I know that no matter how hard I tried, I just didn't measure up to even my own standard of goodness. And then I can't sleep because of the guilt.

You see, I live my days hoping tomorrow will be different. My mind gropes for the answers to my deepest questions; my hand trembles from my attempts to escape reality; my heart aches from the burdens of just keeping on, keeping on. And God, if there is a God, is so far away it doesn't make much difference anyway. Then I die, and they chisel on my gravestone, "Born 1920, Died 1970." And there is only a comma to show for all my hurt, emptiness, loneliness, and suffering.

I walk down a lonely road between a birth and a death. And somewhere down that road, when the loneliness becomes unbearable, I cry out, "Who am I? What am I doing here? Where am I going?" Then I listen, but all I can hear is the cold, dead, hollow, empty silence, and the echo of my questions.

The German philosopher Arthur Schopenhauer, whose pessimistic philosophy rings true to our age, was sitting on a park bench in Berlin one day. He was approached by a curious police officer who asked, "Who are you?"

Schopenhauer, turning momentarily from his thoughts mirrored my problem in his answer. He said, "I wish to God that I knew!"

Science tells me I am a blob of protoplasm. Psychology likens me to a rat running through a maze. Philosophy tries to give me reasons for my running. Historians tell me about my past and statisticians tell me about my future, and I listen. But after they have finished their speeches, there is still the cold, dead, hollow, empty silence. The facts are these: I am paused on a comma between a birth and a death, and I don't know why. I don't even know what the comma is doing there in the first place. I have tried to tie a knot of faith, but it's a slipknot. I am guilty about my past and afraid of my future. I have tried to create meaning from the tangled threads of living, but somebody lost the directions. Camus was right. The only question with which modern man must deal is the question of whether or not he should commit suicide.

This then is the milieu of the world. If it sounds extreme, frightening, and hopeless, that is because it is extreme, frightening, and hopeless. I've been there and I know. The hippie, contrary to what a lot of people think, is not the fool. He has just seen the methods the world uses to gloss over the truth that "life is a long headache on a noisy street," and he refuses to accept those methods. Were God not real, I, too, would try and find meaning in a hippie heaven. The hippie is at least honest— even if he is wrong. Without the Way, the world is bogged down in its own emptiness. Without the Truth, the world will run in meaningless circles. Without the Life, there is a grave at the end of each road.

I want you to go with me on a journey. It isn't a journey just over miles; it is also a journey over time. Our destination, Jerusalem. The year, A.D. 30. As we make our way through a shabby part of Jerusalem, we can hear the sounds of an excited crowd coming from another part of the city, from a street which cuts through the center called in later times the Via Dolorosa. It's a hot day; the air is bittersweet with the smell of desert flowers, drying fruit, and dung fires. There is almost no place one can go to escape the intense heat. With the exception of the shouts of the crowd in the distance, there is an eerie kind of silence which gives one the impression that something wonderful, or something terrible is about to happen.

We make our way through Jerusalem toward the sound of the crowd. Once there, it is difficult to work our way through the mass of people, but when we do the sight before us is enough to shock our senses. There, flanked by soldiers, is a Man stumbling under the weight of a cross. It seems that with each step the Man will fall, but somehow He forces Himself forward toward the Gennath Gate of the city. When He finally does fall, He is kicked, mocked, pushed, and shoved until once again He forces Himself to stumble down the narrow cobblestone street.

One look at this Man's face as He comes near us is enough to filter out the curses of the soldiers and the verbal venom of the crowd. A crown of thorns has been placed on His brow and pressed down until the blood trickles down His face and dries on His half-nude body. As he passes the place where we stand, we can see stripes on His body made earlier by the brutal whip of the soldiers. One can see sharp jabs of pain reflected in the Man's eyes, but there is more there—in His eyes there is pity.

The crowd, the soldiers, and the Man who carries the cross make their way through the streets to a hill in the shape of a skull which is situated outside the wall of the city. They move at such a damnably slow pace we wish they would get the thing over so we could return to our own time and forget it with a cocktail party, a good television show, or some "church work." When they reach the top of the hill, the soldiers push the crowd back. Long nails are driven through the hands and feet of the Man and into the wooden crossbeams. The cross is then hoisted into an already prepared four-foot hole with a *thud* and a cry of agony from the Man who now hangs there. The Man who carried the cross is now carried by the cross.

His death would be slow and painful. For over fourteen hours the Man has received no food or water; He has been beaten and scourged; the loss of blood has drained His limp body of all except the last vestige of life. Those who have come to see the show are not disappointed. Their shrill voices cut through the hot air.

"Hey you," one man shouts, "I thought You were the Son of God. If You are, why don't You come down to us."

"Let's hear some of Your teaching about love now, Son of God," another cried.

Perhaps it was out of fear, or maybe hope that one of the men crucified with the Man joins the crowd. "If You are what You claim to be, save Yourself and us, too."

Those closest to the cross said later that the Man on the cross said, "Father, forgive them for they know not what they do."

And then He died.

That is sad, we say, but what does it have to do with us? Just this, the Man who died on that cross was more than man. In fact, in a unique sense, He was God. On one occasion He said, "I and the Father are one" (John 10:30).

Of course that would seem to be a foolish statement were it not for the fact His disciples who knew Him best, and who had been with Him almost constantly for three years said, not that they had seen a good man die, but that they had seen a dead man walking. They said after He had been hung on the cross, after they had cut His cold, dead cadaver down from the cross, and laid it on a slab of stone, after they had mourned His death for three days—they had seen Him alive. That, too, would seem foolish were it not for the fact that these men were willing to die for that claim. Peter was crucified upside down. All he had to say was, "Look fellows, I made the whole thing up. It really didn't happen." But he didn't. He didn't because it was true. James was run through with the sword. Had he not been so insistent about saying he had seen his Master alive after the cross, they would have let him go.

The disciples' claim would seem foolish until you realize there were a lot of people who had reason to want their claim silenced. You silence a claim that a dead man walked by producing a corpse. Nobody produced a corpse. They couldn't produce one because there was none. There was no corpse because the claim was true.

The disciples' claim would seem foolish until you consider the credibility of the witnesses. Contrary to popular, arrogant thought, the people of the first century were not stupid. It was just as difficult for them to believe a dead man walked as it is for us. However, they had an advantage over us. They could ask the witnesses; they could cross-examine the witnesses; they could probe deeply into the matter to determine the truth. If the witnesses were not good witnesses (i.e. if their case didn't hold water) then Christianity would have died while still in infancy. But Christianity didn't die; it grew and conquered most of the known world by the third century. I submit that it grew and conquered because the witnesses to the resurrection of Christ were telling the truth.

If one takes the time to investigate, one is faced with the inescapable conclusion that the Man who hung on the cross was more than man. He was God, loving the world to a degree that is almost unbelievable.

The question still begs: What does it have to do with me? First, because God loved the world so much He would come to us in His Son and hang on a cross, I can see that a meaningless secular world has been inter- sected with a meaningful sacred world. It is not a pious platitude nor a worn-out slogan. There, for all men to see, is God dying for a world that didn't deserve it. It is from here, and here only, I can draw ultimate meaning. If it is true, the question is no longer one of suicide but a ques- tion of life—life so different and real it must be called abundant. I am no longer a piece of straw caught in the accidental winds of fate. I am not just a blob of proto- plasm, not a rat running through a maze, nor a statistic. I am one who has been loved by a God who came to me, understood me, and died for me. Sometimes when I am tired and lonely, when I wonder why I am wasting my time trying to play God, when I think there is no use, I go and stand on Calvary, and once again I watch God's Son die. I remember, and I am glad.

Secondly, because God loved the world, there is reso- lution for the guilt caused by my compromising with the world. The more I live the more I realize the reality of sin in my own life. My parishioners (at least those who don't know me very well) may think I am good and kind. The people in the community are easily fooled because I'm a minister, and ministers are supposed to be good and kind. Sometimes I can even fool my family. But I can't fool myself. What's more important, I can't forgive myself. But "God has done what the law, weakened by the flesh, could not do: sending his own Son in the likeness of sinful flesh and for sin, he condemned sin in the flesh, in order that the just requirement of the law might be fulfilled in us, who walk not according to the flesh but according to the Spirit" (Romans 8:2–4). When, in the quietness of my solitude, I confront the essential failure of my efforts to live according to God's commands, I go and stand on Calvary, and once again I watch God's Son die. I remember, and I am glad.

Because God's world would enter my world and manifest itself on a cross, I am able to love. Love is just not my nature, and that fact causes my loneliness. I have no love for those who don't love me. Mrs. Jones who is always using the minister as her own bellhop, Mr. Brown who would rather see the church bank account grow than to see lives changed, the man in the two-room apartment infested with rats who has no answer when his children ask, "Why?"—these are the people I try to avoid because I'm not capable of loving them. I'm not capable of loving because I haven't been loved either. That is, until I go and see God's Son die on a cross for me. Then His love is born in me and manifests itself through me.

God's Son dying on a cross also speaks to me about the final triumph of His world over my world. We did our worst. He was given all of the hate, bitterness, and hurt our world could give. He was rejected, slandered, mocked, and then He was laid to rest. We thought we were rid of Him but our tombs were not strong enough; His love was stronger than our hate. When He got up out of His tomb, He became a sign that points to the final culmination of the battle between His world and mine. He calls me to a winning side, and I have followed, trusting to Him my life and my death for He said, " ... be of good cheer, I have overcome the world" (John 16:33).

It is popular today for one (especially if he happens to be a young minister) to say the church has drawn an artificial distinction between the sacred and the secular. Because of this artificial distinction, many say, the church has found itself in the embarrassing position of being both irrelevant and unfaithful. The secular city is really the sacred city. The city just doesn't know it yet. When the church finally discovers the sacredness of the city, they say, we can proceed to the more important business of informing the city of the fact. "He's got the whole world in His hands," and that makes the whole world sacred. Everyone can now join hands and walk off into the sunset together.

All of this would be fine except for one thing. It isn't true. The distinction between sacred and secular isn't artificial. If the church is irrelevant and unfaithful, it isn't because it drew an artificial line; if anything, it is because it drew the line in the wrong place. The Bible makes a distinction between sacred and secular, Christian and non-Christian, church and world. Only a cursory glance at the Scriptures will convince all, except those who don't want to be confused with the facts, that the artificial distinction isn't artificial at all. It is real. John's statement is clear: "Do not love the world or the things in the world. If anyone loves the world, love for the Father is not in him. For all that is in the world, the lust of the flesh and the lust of the eyes and the pride of life, is not of the Father but is of the world" (I John 2:15–16). It is a Biblical distinction, and we would do well to heed it.

There are those who say by Christ's coming into our world we are shown the essential sacredness of the world. But that isn't true. By His coming we are shown the true nature of our world which is secular. We are shown that no matter how much you try to cover it up with meaningless conversation and colorful posters, it is still a dark, frightening place. Jesus said, "I am the light of the world; he who follows me will not walk in darkness, but will have the light of life" (John 8:12). Jesus at this point is not only saying something about Himself; He is saying something about the world. If He is the light of the world, then without Him the world is dark. If He provides light for those who would follow Him, then those who don't follow Him will walk in the dark. A distinction made by Jesus over and over again is the distinction between His world and ours.

The question then is this: Where does one draw the line? A lot of people draw it in the wrong place. For instance, they see members of the Ladies Aid sewing blankets for missionaries as a sacred act, while they see a group of businessmen working on an important business problem as a secular act. If that is what some mean by "artificial distinction" then I would agree. The difficulty at this point is seeing sacred and secular in terms of actions (e.g. smoking, drinking) and things (e.g. cigarettes, liquor). If one's view becomes this narrow, then things such as cars and planes and actions such as working and playing are classed under a secular heading. Attending worship services, praying, and singing hymns would fall in the sacred column.

However, when the Bible draws a line between that which is sacred and that which is secular, it is done in terms of attitude. Jesus said, " ... the cares of the world and the delight in riches choke the word, and it proves unfruitful" (Matthew 13:22). John said, "Do not love the world or the things in the world" (I John 2:15). Paul said, "And you he made alive, when you were dead through the trespasses and sins in which you once walked, following the course of this world, following the prince of the power of the air, the spirit that is now at work in the sons of disobedience" (Ephesians 2:1-2). Thus, one can see the man who is working in business and consciously honoring his God by that work may be acting in a sacred fashion more than the lady who sews blankets and gossips between stitches. The difference is one of attitude— where one places one's love—not of actions or things. To be *in and not of* the world is to act in every area of your life so as to make that action sacred.

This principle, however, cannot be separated from certain actions and things. There are acts which tend to make it impossible to honor God. For instance, the actions of a drunk make it difficult for him to honor God. Sex, when it becomes perverted (i.e. when it turns inward on itself for only selfish gratification), is of the world. One cannot call adultery sacred. The businessman who will make a dollar by any means possible is working in the secular. I don't want to labor the point, but you can see the principle: With only certain exceptions, "sacred" and "secular" are defined in terms of one's relationship to actions and things rather than by the actions and things themselves.

With all of the above as groundwork what then is the relationship of the Christian to the world? First, the Christian is not to be conformed to the world (Romans 12:2). If you will let it, the world will try and force you into its mold. The world shouts at the Christian, "Don't make waves; take it easy; to get along you must go along." If you will let it, the world will try to rob you of your Lord. It will tell you that in order to be accepted by the crowd you must say certain things, read certain books, snub certain people, live in a certain neighborhood, and revere certain gods.

A woman told me recently that all her life she had been doing things because those things were expected of her. "And now," she said, "I don't know how to stop."

It is easy to be conformed to the world. You give a little here and a little there, and soon God doesn't matter anymore. I've been there, and I know how easy it is. There was a time when making a dollar was the most important thing in my life, when I would do anything to please the crowd, when I made an effort to be narrow, negative, and nauseating because it was popular to be narrow, negative, and nauseating. A Christian is not to be conformed to this world.

Second, a Christian is not to be in love with the world. "If any man loves the world, love for the Father is not in him" (I John 2:15). Often a couple will come to me to discuss their marriage plans. You can always see the stars

84

in their eyes. He sees her as a wonderful, enchanting princess. She sees him as a knight in bright, shining armor. Each believes the other to be without faults. Although this is a form of love, it is not the real thing. It is infatuation, and over a long period it will, one hopes, develop into love. Love for the world develops in the same fashion. It doesn't happen overnight; it begins with infatuation.

For instance, a man may say as he starts his business career, "I am not really interested in getting rich. All I want is enough to be comfortable, take care of my family, and pay the bills." But as the years go by, and he is comfortable, and can take care of his family, and pay the bills, he finds money has achieved the status of a god. Money, no longer a means to an end, becomes a goal in itself. I have a friend who decided that a little fling outside his marriage wouldn't hurt anyone. When I got to know him, he had made a practice of going from bar to girl with a passion that was all consuming. He made every effort to stop, but his infatuation had developed into a love. I watched him cry one night, and I knew he was living in a literal hell. When anything in my life comes before God, I have placed my love in the wrong place. It can be business, or church, or social work, or family, but whatever, it can destroy my fellowship with God. A Christian is not to love the world.

But admonitions of Scripture are not always negative. A Christian is supposed to be a light to the world. Jesus said, "You are the light of the world" (Matthew 5:14). This statement, in itself, implies a vast difference between a Christian and a non-Christian, between the church and the world. Whereas the Christian and the church constitute light, the world constitutes darkness. For instance, there is the light of truth. Christians have been given a truth that transcends the systems of man. The truth that God has come to man in His Son, and loved man, and redeemed man is a light which the Christian is supposed to shine into the darkness of the world. There is also the light of freedom. Most people are in terrible bondage to their rut, their lies, and their sin. Jesus has set the Christian free. That freedom is a light and a sign to the world that beyond themselves there is a Source that sets men free. Finally, there is the light of love. Real love for the hurt, the oppressed, the lonely, the bound, the unlovely, and the lost is a gift from God. It is not the nature of man to love. In just the fact that the Christian possesses a supernatural ability to love, new light is shed into the darkness of the world.

A Christian is also to be as salt to the world. Jesus said, "You are the salt of the earth ... " (Matthew 5:13). Salt is a preservative. The difference between a Christian and the world ought to be seen in the sticking power of the Christian. When other reformers have gone home to bed, when the band-wagon jumpers have grown tired of the ride, when the flaming pseudoprophets have decided it isn't worth the effort, it will be the Christian who stays in the battle. He will stay because he is acting out of obedience and not emotion. That is how the Christian is different from the world.

Salt also adds zest to the food to which it is added. There is a quality about a Christian which is different; it is an inner quality of joy and purpose. When the world sees that quality, the world will know somewhere there is Someone who makes keeping on worth the effort. That is how the Christian is different from the world.

Salt doesn't call attention to itself. When a Christian has found out who he is, and what he is doing here, he does not pat himself on the back and congratulate himself on his insight. He knows better. He knows his Source is not himself but his Lord. He lives under the conviction that grace is not manufactured but accepted. He knows he is not self-made but God-made. That is why he is different from the world.

Salt is effective far out of proportion to its size and volume. Jesus started a revolution with only twelve followers, and one of those betrayed Him. But God knows no minority, and because of these men, the world will never be the same. Their lives, because of the Holy Spirit, knew no bounds of effectiveness. That is the difference between the Christian and the world.

The difference between sacred and secular, between Church and world, and between Christian and non-Christian is Biblical and real. When we realize it, perhaps the Christian church will stop trying to play the world's game; perhaps the Christian church will stop trying to become so relevant that no one can taste the salt or see the light. When the difference is realized, perhaps the church will once again become what the Greek word for "church" means—"called-out ones." When we stop listening to the world to the exclusion of our Lord, then the different drummer will once again beat the cadence of salvation.

Why do you suppose Paul said Christians should not be conformed to the world? Why do you think Jesus said we ought to be different? Because they wanted Christians to wall themselves off from their object of mission? Because they believed Christianity survives best in a cloistered environment? Because they were afraid Christians might have too much fun? Of course not! They realized when a man becomes Christian he is a new creation. They realized there is something different and distinct about him, something that won't go into the world's mold. They knew if you put "new wine into old wineskins" you could lose both the wine and the wineskins.

The Christians were lined up for battle. Their Leader was giving final instructions. "You are to win the market-place in My name," He said. "You will have to carry a cross, and you will sometimes be tired and lonely. But if you love Me and each other you will find power. If you go forth in My name and under the power of My Spirit, the marketplace will be won. If you persist in this work, the fruit of your labor will be worth the tiredness, the loneliness, and the cross."

As the Christians broke ranks there was determination in their faces and courage in their hearts. The Master had spoken, and they would be obedient. As the Christians approached the marketplace, a joyous shout arose from their ranks. Soon, using the weapons of the Spirit, they would bring the marketplace to its knees before the Master. But as the Christians entered the gates of the marketplace, their attention was diverted from their task to the harsh bark of the con men, the bright wares of the peddlers, and the skill of the actors.

Meanwhile, the Leader waited on a hill outside the walls of the marketplace. Days passed without any sign of the Christians, and the Leader, thinking something terrible must have happened, decided to investigate. When He entered the marketplace, He inquired if anyone had seen the Christians. Some remembered their entrance; others recalled their shouts of joy as they came through the gate, but no one remembered what had happened to them. It was only a short time until the Leader realized what had happened. He couldn't find Christians because He couldn't tell them from the con men, the peddlers, and the actors!

5

THE TASK

But you shall receive power when the Holy Spirit has come upon you; and you shall be my witnesses in Jerusalem and in all Judea and Samaria and to the end of the earth.

ACTS 1:8

IF THERE IS ANYTHING about which all of the factions in the church can agree, it is this: something must be done. The day when the church could rest and wait, secure in the knowledge it was accepted and loved, is long past. The church is accepted by a rapidly decreasing number of people, and it is loved less than it is accepted. Our problem is that we are still resting and waiting. I don't rejoice in that fact, but, nevertheless, it is still a fact. Not too long ago a young friend of mine told me, "I don't hate the church; the people in the church are, I suppose, doing their thing. I just don't care." That kind of statement bothers me because I am a young man who has given the rest of his life to service in the church of Jesus Christ. If the church should die, or even become terminally sick, not only am I out of a job, I am also minus a dream.

I could understand if the situation were dictated by either the lack of need on the part of the world or the lack of resource on the part of the church, but neither is true. If ever the world needed to find a correct diagnosis for its problems, it is now. If ever the world needed to discover how to love away the hurt, bridge the brokenness, and resolve the guilt, it is now. There is a meaningless paganism in the world which needs a challenge. Salvation is the name of the game, and if the church can't deliver then I ought to be out of a job, and the dream doesn't make much difference anyway.

On the day before I was ordained there was a retreat for those of us who would henceforth preface our names with a "Reverend." During that retreat we were discussing a particular problem and how we, as ministers, would handle the problem. I don't remember the problem, but I do remember what one person said in reference to it. He gave us a smug, knowing smile and said, "I would tell him that I cannot be an answer man." Well, we had better learn to be answer men and women in the church! The world is looking for some answers, and their questions won't wait. If we tell the world we aren't "answer men," they will not see our intellectual honesty. They will assume, and quite rightly, either we don't have any answers, or the secret isn't worth the effort. Would that God might give us some answers!

I am a minister in the church because I believe the church has some answers. I believe our problem is one of realizing the answers are there, they can be real to us, and they must be given to the world. So far, we are agreed something must be done. That means to many of us we aren't sure there are answers to the world's questions, we haven't found them, and it would be useless to try and fake it. Mark Twain, through a character in his story, "The Mysterious Stranger," has expressed the way many honest clerics feel. "It is true, that which I have revealed to you; there is no God, no universe, no human race, no earthly life, no heaven, no hell. It is all a dream —a grotesque and foolish dream. Nothing exists but you. And you are but a thought—a vagrant thought, a useless thought, a homeless thought, wandering forlorn among the empty eternities!"

The question then is this: What in the world are we doing here? Jesus had an answer, and it's just as true today as it was when He gave it. "But you shall receive power when the Holy Spirit has come upon you; and you shall be my witnesses in Jerusalem and in all Judea and Samaria and to the end of the earth" (Acts 1:8). The church's business, its only business, is to witness to Jesus Christ. When we don't—we aren't. It's that simple.

That sounds good, but what does it mean? A witness is a person who points to someone or something in a manner that will illumine. Thus, when you tell friends about a movie or a book, you become a witness. When a person with whom I have been playing golf tells another person about my score, he becomes a witness. Every day of our lives we witness to something. The problem with many of us in the church is that we have been witnessing to the wrong thing. When we witness to anything other than Jesus Christ, we have failed in our task. No matter how efficient we are in raising money or filling pews, if that is our witness, we have missed the point of our existence. If our preaching, social action, and psychological insights say nothing to the world except that we talk, act, and understand, then there is a gap between Jesus' commandment and our response. If the church produces scholars because scholarship is a good thing, or musicians because music is nice, or thinkers because everybody ought to think, it may be laudable, but it isn't what Jesus told us to do. He told us we were to be His witnesses.

One of the most helpful ways to understand Jesus' admonition to be His witnesses is to relate the concept to a witness in a court of law. For instance, a witness in a court of law must be available for the trial. Recently, in my state, an important trial was called off because the star witness was killed. That can happen in the church. The world has put Christianity on trial, but too many of the witnesses have fled.

Most people don't care what the church believes. They will never read a Bible and many will never sit in a pew. They could care less about the budget or the building. But somewhere they have gotten the idea that a Christian ought to be different. They assume an active member of the church has found something or he wouldn't continue as a church member. Mr. Pagan is looking at Mr. Christian and hoping he will find a witness to something which is better than the emptiness. But when he looks he often finds the man he expected to be different is just as lonely, afraid, and frustrated as he is. He sees a man who will talk about anything—his golf score, his country club, his new car, his job—but not his faith. He sees racism as real as his own. He sees anger and hate peering through the saintly smile, and he figures the witness has died. You see, when we say we believe the omnipotent, omnipresent, omniscient God who created and sustained the universe has entered man's history and died on a cross to make us free, and then don't say or do anything about it, anyone with a lick of sense will know we really don't believe it. Then the witness will have failed to show up for the trial, and that is sad because the evidence is so strong if somebody would just present it.

Also, in a court of law, a witness must have something to witness. In other words, if a witness has nothing to say the court is wasting its time. If the evidence is hearsay, it won't be accepted. It is sad but true many of us in the church don't have anything to say except hearsay. To say Jesus Christ came to save the world is something quite different than saying Jesus Christ came and saved me. Christianity must begin at home or it won't begin.

One of the distinguishing marks of the New Testament church was the use of the personal. They didn't say, "We have heard Jesus Christ is man's salvation from helplessness." They didn't say, "We have it on good authority God will free us from sin." They didn't say, "We believe Jesus Christ provides joy." They said, "We have experienced hope and freedom, and we are joyful!" That's why the world listened! The church needs to pray for revival. When that comes, we will have something to say.

Finally, a witness must be able to stand up under cross-examination. Perry Mason always had a way of getting to the truth. If a someone was lying, Mason would find out. Well, the world makes Perry Mason look like a first-year law student. A phony Christian will not last long when the world checks out his testimony. He may be able to talk a good fight, but that won't do when the going gets rough. The world will see behind the mask when the hungry aren't fed, and the dead aren't raised. Phony resurrections just don't happen, and food isn't produced with words. The battle rages, and the man who stays in the rear talking about how well he fights will get and deserve only laughter.

In the church I once served, we had a little boy in the church school who came from a family with serious problems. Because of those, he was a problem. Whenever the teacher tried to talk to the children, he would do everything in his power to distract the class. He opposed every suggestion made by the teacher. He refused to cooperate with anyone. One day, in the midst of a temper tantrum, he slapped his teacher. Forcing herself to keep from getting angry, she threw her arms around the boy and said, "That's all right Billy, I love you anyway." Her testimony stood up under cross-examination, and the little boy's life from that day on showed it. Jesus Christ, for the first time in the boy's life, was real. He had seen Jesus in a woman who loved him when he didn't deserve it.

How does one witness? It isn't enough to say a witness must show up for the trial, have something to witness and be able to bear up under cross-examination. One must find a way to witness so as to illumine Jesus Christ. A witness can show up at the trial and be of no possible use; he can have an experience to witness and be so inarticulate that it won't make any difference; he can stand up under cross-examination but have a testimony which isn't worth cross-examination.

First, one is a witness because of what one believes. We live in a time of tolerance. It doesn't matter what you believe, some say, as long as you believe something and are sincere about it. That isn't true. It *does* matter what you believe. If fact, what you believe will make you what you are. If you believe in child sacrifice, for instance, that belief will work its way out in some rather antisocial behavior. If you believe God is a God who sits in the heavens ready to zap anyone who dares to disobey Him, then you are going to live a life of fear and guilt. If you believe God is Santa Claus who doesn't really care about your sin, you will not bother to consider His opinion. If you are a deist you will act differently than you would if you were a theist. It does matter what you believe. Paul said, "For man believes with his heart and so is justified, and he confesses with his lips and so is saved." (Romans 10:10). In other words what you believe will be reflected in what you are.

There are people in the church who say we need to set aside our beliefs and join hands to work for a better world. Our problem, they say, is that we get "hung up" on doctrines and dogmas when we ought to be out on the firing line. That sounds good, but it is the philosophy of a man who has not examined the facts. You don't join hands and work for a better world unless you believe something strongly enough to make you care that there is a better world. Nobody is going to pull me away from my comfortable existence and put me on the firing line unless there is some belief within me which makes me think I ought to be there. When I was a boy, I am told the barber made me sit still in his chair by pecking on the wall and telling me that devils were in there. I assumed that I had better be still or else! The belief I held caused my behavior to take a turn for the better.

Because I believe Jesus Christ is the God-man, because I believe He has chosen me, because I believe He is active in the world, because I believe He loves, my posture as a witness is quite different than it would be if I

96

believed none of these things. Because I believe the Scriptures to be the infallible rule for my life, I am placed in the position of obedience to that which I read and understand. When my belief reflects the truth (i.e. when I believe true things) I become a faithful witness, and my life shows it.

One is a witness by what one is. Jesus said, "And you shall *be* my witnesses. . . . " A Christian is not just another person; he is a particular person. Paul said, "Therefore, if any one is in Christ, he is a new creation; the old has passed away, behold, the new has come" (II Corinthians 5:17). In other words, there is something about a Christian which is new to the world. The Christian, by just being a Christian, reflects the love, understanding, and care of Jesus. When I was younger and my friends and I would plan to do something which was outside the bounds of proper action as the law saw it, just the sight of a policeman walking his beat was enough to bring our planned actions within those proper bounds. He didn't have to say or do anything; he just had to be there and that was enough. It is the same way with the Christian. Just the presence of one who loves in the midst of a hostile situation is enough to transform the situation. You would be suprised at how fast our sand-lot baseball team would clean up the language when one of the Christian fellows would come on the scene. A church can be completely transformed by a group of faithful, committed Christians who are just there. It is important in the racially tense situations which are all too common in our country that there be the presence of Christians, not necessarily doing or saying something, but just being in Christ and in the situation.

97

When I first entered the ministry, I was called to the home of a woman who had lost her husband in an automobile accident. I was so frightened I couldn't think, much less talk. I mumbled a few words about being sorry and then just sat there. I was too frightened to say anything that would comfort or to do anything that would help. Weeks later the woman thanked me for my help and comfort during the time of her bereavement. I told her I had done nothing deserving her thanks. I said that I had probably made things worse. "No, Mr. Brown," she said, "you were there and that was enough." The Christian is a witness to Jesus Christ by just being.

A Christian is a witness by what he does. Someone was asked under whose preaching he was converted. "By no man's preaching," he said, "but by a mother's practicing." Many people can testify that before they heard the Gospel they saw the Gospel working through the actions of a Christian. This is why it is important that, insofar as possible, Christian missionaries should have a skill which can be given to those to whom they minister. A man who is able to heal bodies with his God-given talent is going to say something to people his words could never say. A missionary who brings knowledge through her skills as a teacher will be a witness to Jesus and His love as much as anything she could say.

When a Christian talks about the love of Jesus and refuses to do anything about racism, his witness will be false. When we talk about the hunger of the heart without doing anything about the hunger of the stomach, we cease to be a witness for Jesus. The whole twenty-fifth chapter of Matthew is enough to make a talk-oriented Christian wince. Especially to the point are the words of

Jesus to those who refused to act. " 'Depart from me, you cursed, into the eternal fire prepared for the devil and his angels; for I was hungry and you gave me no food, I was thirsty and you gave me no drink, I was a stranger and you did not welcome me, naked and you did not clothe me, sick and in prison and you did not visit me.' Then they also will answer, 'Lord, when did we see thee hungry or thirsty or a stranger or naked or sick or in prison, and did not minister to thee?' Then he will answer them, 'Truly, I say to you, as you did it not to one of the least of these, you did it not to me.' " (Matthew 25:41–45). We are a witness to the world by what we do.

Finally, we are witnesses by what we say. It is true that often "what you are speaks louder than what you say." It is true we ought to be a witness with our actions; but for a lot of people the witness of action is an excuse for ignoring the need for a witness of words. There is no way in the world for a Christian to tell another person about the cross of Jesus Christ by being good. The person to whom the witness is made will say, "My, he sure is a good person." Perhaps he might even say, "I bet that he is religious." But, according to the Bible, that isn't enough. Mr. Pagan will not find what he needs by emulating Mr. Christian's goodness or his religiosity. Mr. Pagan needs to be told about his sin, his need, his end, and his Saviour. He must have someone who is articulate enough to communicate the experience of Christ with words.

My wife is a musician, and she always says music is the universal language. Now that is true depending on what you are trying to say with the music. If you are trying to communicate a mood, a feeling or an aesthetic experience then perhaps music is the universal language. However, if you want to talk about how the Gestalt school of psychology stresses the integral and relational character of psychic phenomena (whatever that means) then you can't do it with Bach. It is the same with Christianity. The goodness produced by Christ in the lives of Christians is not a universal language. If one wants to really point to Jesus then one must move beyond deeds of goodness to words.

When I was in seminary nobody told me what to say to the man or woman who comes to me and asks, "How do I become a Christian?" In fact, I was not told anybody would be even asking a question like that. I knew they would be asking questions about theological concepts, and I was prepared to make an answer. I understood there would be people who would come to me with psychological problems, and I learned how to deal with those problems. As a future administrative officer in the church, they told me I would have to answer questions dealing with fund raising, organizational structure, and program involvement. I have some answers to those kinds of questions. But nobody told me what to say to the man who is seeking Christ. Nobody told me there were people in the church who, more than anything else, want to make the theological concepts experiential facts. I was not told there are people for whom it is more important to have their name on the Book of Life than the church roll.

In the short time I have been a minister, I have become aware that there is a terrible deficiency among laymen in the area of expressing their faith with words. There is a crying need for laymen who are not only told to act uprightly, but who are also trained to be articulate about the things they have experienced. We need laymen who are able to lead others to Christ with actions and words. We need members of the church who will stand up and speak up. One becomes a witness with one's words.

The problem with all of the above is that, even if it is utilized, it is still likely to meet with failure. There is the missing ingredient that, when added, transforms words and deeds into effective communication. That ingredient is the Holy Spirit. We have a problem with those to whom the church must witness, "For Jews demand signs and Greeks seek wisdom, but we preach Christ crucified, a stumbling block to Jews and folly to Gentiles ... " (I Corinthians 1:22–23). That which seems to be "a stumbling block" to some and "folly" to others is not likely to inspire a life commitment. The power which does inspire commitment is the Holy Spirit. Jesus said, "But you shall receive power when the Holy Spirit has come upon you ... " (Acts 1:8).

One Sunday morning recently I preached a sermon on witness, making reference to the Holy Spirit. While I was speaking on this point, I noticed the blank faces of the people in the congregation and realized I had served this church for almost two years and had never preached a sermon on the Holy Spirit. How tragic! However, my failure is not isolated. I believe there are many ministers who have too little to say about the Holy Spirit. I also believe that here lies much of the reason for the lack of power in the church today.

The doctrine of the Holy Spirit is not a doctrine

dreamed up in the spare time of first century theologians. It is a doctrine created to explain and communicate a vital experience. The early church had experienced a work in their lives which had given them supernatural power. The members of the early church had been given different gifts of the Spirit which enabled them, when working together, to become a body operating in the fulness of health. Jesus had promised them they would receive power when the Holy Spirit had come upon them. When they received that power their lives were never the same. The Holy Spirit led, convicted, empowered, revealed, and comforted. When the experience of being led by God to the places where He wants us is missing, the doctrine of the Holy Spirit is not necessary. When people are not convicted of sin and are not revealed spiritual truth, then there is no need for a doctrine of the Holy Spirit which will explain conviction and revelation. When there is no power and no comfort, questions regarding the Holy Spirit are mute questions. Maybe that is why we have been saying so little about the Holy Spirit.

Another reason I think the Holy Spirit is so easily forgotten is the fact that you can't force Him into an ecclesiastical mold nor channel Him into a program. The Holy Spirit moves where He wills, and that bothers those of us who want to keep our "hands on the strings." The reactions of many clerics to the modern-day charismatic renewal illustrate how easily we can be threatened by something we don't understand. We find laymen talking about the Holy Spirit when we haven't even preached on it. We see life in places we haven't programed. We see men and women who are "on fire" and it doesn't fit our theological molds. It is enough to make us ministers feel we aren't needed!

Whenever God has caused revival in His church, there has been much talk about the Holy Spirit. People are beginning to talk. Perhaps now is the time. You see, the Holy Spirit is to the church and to individual Christians what gasoline is to an automobile or electricity is to an iron. It is that which takes our half-baked actions and our halting words, rubs them together and makes a fire. If we ministers would just stop whining for a moment, we might smell smoke.

When people in the church get on their knees and pray for a fresh visitation of the Holy Spirit, God will show us the tasks with which He will help us. One of the reasons the church is so busy with so little result is that we are often busy at those tasks which we try to do by ourselves. If we would but watch God at work, go where He is and help, we would be surprised at how successful we might become. When that happens we can call it the Holy Spirit.

When people in the church pray for the Holy Spirit, God will show us what is wrong in our lives and will convict those in the world of that which is wrong in their lives. Our difficulty has often been that we think we have no sin and our purpose in the world is to show *them* how to be like *us*. If we could ever realize that the "saints" need some cleaning up, too, the world would realize that maybe we have a point. If that happens, we can call it the Holy Spirit.

If we would only pray for the Holy Spirit, God would work through us, and we would stand amazed in the presence of His power. The people of the early church were constantly expecting a miracle. Their expectations were seldom disappointed. They were like little children waiting to see where God would surprise them next. The lame threw away their crutches and danced. The hardened hearts of the multitudes were penetrated with the cross of Christ. When was the last time you saw a miracle? When you do, you can call it the Holy Spirit.

If we would pray for the Holy Spirit, God would reveal to us some truths we heretofore have ignored. It might dawn on us there are things which can't be explained with our categories. We might find that Jesus knew what He was talking about when He talked about the supernatural. We might find there are spiritual laws which aren't taught in Physics 101. Too often we have thought of truth in terms of a syllogism. God may have something new to teach us and when that happens, we can call it the Holy Spirit.

Sincere prayers for the Holy Spirit coming from the lips of Christians might bring to our lives a comfort we have never known. Anxiety is the modern-day mark of the church. We are a comfortless people, and it shouldn't be that way. The problem is that it is hard to do the work you are supposed to do when you can't rest; it's hard to obey the commandments of Christ if there is too much grief beside open graves and too many tears beside open wounds. God will comfort His people and when He does, you call it the Holy Spirit.

When one considers what the results of the church's witness ought to be, the New Testament church is the prototype. It is here one finds success defined in God's terms and in terms which ought to be applicable to the modern-day church. For instance, when we in the church of today are successful with the church fair, it isn't necessarily because God was working through the fair. When we have a new stewardship program which raises the per-member giving by eighty percent, it isn't necessarily because this is the expected result of our witness. These aren't the terms by which the New Testament defines successful results. If we are faithful in our witness, certain manifestations of that faithfulness ought to take place.

As one reads through the New Testament, one is impressed with the way the Christian faith spread. As people heard the good news of Jesus Christ, they, too, were caught up in the stream of believers. The very first witness that was given after the coming of the Holy Spirit at Pentecost bore fruit. "Now when they heard this they were cut to the heart, and said to Peter and the rest of the apostles, 'Brethren, what shall we do?' And Peter said to them, 'Repent, and be baptized every one of you in the name of Jesus Christ for the forgiveness of your sins; and you shall receive the gift of the Holy Spirit. For the promise is to you and to your children and to all that are far off, every one whom the Lord our God calls to him . . . ' So those who received his word were baptized, and there were added that day about three thousand souls" (Acts 2:37–41). Everywhere the witnesses of Jesus went—prison, royal courts, philosophical forums—their message was heard and accepted. That which was accepted, it must be remembered, was not a theological position nor an ecclesiastical system, but the Person of Jesus Christ.

When we in the church see our witness is not bearing

the same kind of fruit, we ought to ask ourselves some serious questions. If three thousand souls were added to the church I serve because of only one witness I would be hysterical, the denominational headquarters would send a letter to the officers of my church requesting I be given a battery of psychological tests, and those who were less kind would say I had somehow juggled the figures. But it should not be that way! We ought to expect and see this kind of thing happening all the time.

People were not only brought to Christ, they were brought together. After the witness of Peter following Pentecost, Luke tells us, "And they devoted themselves to the apostles' teaching and fellowship, to the breaking of bread and prayers" (Acts 2:42). Fellowship in the early church was not only the result of the witness, it was also one of the keys to further results. As one reads through the Gospels, one is impressed by the fact that Jesus formed a fellowship, trained a fellowship, and commissioned a fellowship. You see, Jesus knew if He sent out individuals they would fail. Thomas had so many doubts he could never have been effective. James and John would have ended up fighting over who would be the bishop. Peter would have started cursing and pushing until he forced potential converts into submission. But together these men, who would have failed individually, turned the world upside down. They knew that in the world they would be persecuted, but they also knew back home they had Christian brothers who cared and understood. They knew in the world they would be hated and scorned, but they also knew back home there were friends with whom they could be honest and open, with whom they could find strength to keep on keeping

106

on. It was this fellowship which provided the soil from which the church of Christ grew.

As people in the church become faithful in their witness, fellowship is the natural result because the closer we draw to Jesus the nearer we are to each other. This phenomenon of fellowship becomes a circle of power from which new commitments are made and new fellowship is established. One of the most exciting movements in the church today is the small group movement in which people are finding fresh power and purpose together in Jesus Christ.

Another result of a faithful witness is that the impossible becomes possible. In the third chapter of Acts, Peter and John were going up to the temple at the hour of prayer. There was a lame begger who asked for money. "But Peter said, 'I have no silver and gold, but I give you what I have; in the name of Jesus Christ of Nazareth, walk.' And he took him by the right hand and raised him up; and immediately his feet and ankles were made strong. And leaping up he stood and walked and entered the temple with them, walking and leaping and praising God" (Acts 3:6–8). Today most of us would say that either the man was a hypochondriac or he would have gotten well anyway. Therein lies one of our difficulties. If you had been in the early church and someone had prayed for the ceiling to fall, you would have crawled under a chair. Prison doors were opened, the sick were healed, and nations were moved because the church knew all things were possible. Today even the possible is impossible because we aren't willing to accept the active intervention of God in the work of the church. We would rather depend on public relations and money. May God forgive us!

Because of the faithful witness of the New Testament

church, there was an outpouring of love and compassion. When Stephen was being stoned to death he prayed, "Lord, do not hold this sin against them" (Acts 7:60). Peter was able to break the barrier of pride. A Jew by birth, he considered himself superior to the Gentiles, and yet he went to them with these words. "You yourselves know how unlawful it is for a Jew to associate with or to visit anyone of another nation; but God has shown me that I should not call any man common or unclean. So when I was sent for, I came without objection" (Acts 10:28). In the twenty-seventh chapter of Acts, the apostle Paul is a prisoner on a ship sailing to Rome. Notice his compassion and love for those who hold him prisoner. Why do you suppose Stephen was able to pray for his enemies, Peter was able to break his pride, and Paul was able to show compassion to his jailers? Because the natural result of their faithfulness to Jesus Christ was love and compassion. If the church of today were to have that same compassion and love, there would be no question about social concern and racial reconciliation. Both would be the interest we would collect on our witness.

Because of the witness of the early church, the church itself was built up. "So the church throughout all Judea and Galilee and Samaria had peace and was built up; and walking in the fear of the Lord and in the comfort of the Holy Spirit it was multiplied" (Acts 9:31). Just as you lose happiness if you pursue it, so the church loses statistical success if it pursues numbers. The interesting thing about the early church was that it wasn't always looking for a program to bring renewal; they weren't busy trying to understand the fall in membership; they didn't care about their annual report. They just did their business and trusted God for the harvest. We need to learn that lesson. Many denominations in the United States have seen drastic falls in membership and giving in recent years. Perhaps the reason for the drastic fall is our interest in membership and giving rather than in witnessing to our Lord. The natural result of a faithful witness is the building up of the church. If the church isn't built up, we ought to be concerned about our witness and not the process of building up.

Robert Coleman, in his book *The Master Plan of Evangelism,* sums up the issue: "The world is desperately seeking someone to follow. That they will follow someone is certain, but will he be a man who knows the way of Christ, or will he be one like themselves leading them only on into greater darkness?

"This is the decisive question. . . . The revelance of all that we do waits upon its verdict, and in turn, the destiny of the multitudes hangs in the balance."

6

THE FUTURE

I am the Alpha and the Omega, ... the
beginning and the end.

REVELATION 22:13

I AM A YOUNG MAN with a future. It is a future so exciting and wonderful it defies description. Not only do I have a future which is exciting and wonderful, so does the organization for which I work. How do I know? I know because the One who controls the future controls me and the organization for which I work. He is the beginning and the end of everything, and He doesn't make mistakes. History moves at His command. There are no surprises to Him, and there is no anxiety in Him. You can talk about the final destruction of mankind at the hands of an atomic monster; you can talk about how the world rocks on the edge of the precipice; you can talk about the ultimate victory of communism or capitalism; you can whine about how the world's problems have no solutions, but I know better. When the last page of history has been turned and the historians are dead, the One in whom I have put my trust and for whom I have committed my life will stand victorious. It's already decided. The future begins now, and it doesn't stop.

I used to think the future depended on men and their willingness to protect and preserve civilization. If men would just realize the problems then the future would be safe. Education would build the roads, and reason would travel those roads to a world where hate would be abolished, and love would prevail. Rational men would build a rational world where humankind would live in peace and brotherhood. If men would only realize the problems, spears could be used for pruning hooks and swords for plowshares.

But, as I grew a little older and wiser, my bright world of tomorrow fell to pieces. Men did realize the problems, but they didn't do anything about them. In fact, politicians used the problems to obtain votes, opportunists manipulated the problems for a fast dollar, and the ordinary man preferred to watch television. Education built a few roads, but its bombs were always better than its roads. As I looked at the world of tomorrow, I saw reason giving way to unreasoned hate. I saw love becoming only a word with which the promoters advertised the latest movie. I saw peace and brotherhood were mostly words used by men who understood that if there was no hope, there was nothing. I saw the appearance of man could have been only an accident and man's destruction could come in the same way. At any time the past could catch up with the present and wipe out the future.

A friend of mine once told me, "Steve, you had better live now, because there may not be a tomorrow." I suppose the conversation which took place in a small upper room in Jerusalem after the death of Jesus of Nazareth had similar overtones. The men who had

111

gathered in that small room had seen their hopes shattered when their Leader died on a cross crying His God had forsaken Him. Only a week before these men had a future. That future had died when Jesus died, and you could see it in their faces. It was a classic study in despair. The work and dreams of three years were now dead, on a cold slab of stone, in somebody else's tomb.

These men would return to their old lives sadder but wiser men. Memories—empty, lonely, haunting memories—were all they had now, and for men who had possessed so much more, memories were little consolation. They would remember the times when the Master would bend His big frame over to listen to a child whisper in His ear. They would remember the sound of beggar's cups clanking against the rocks beside the road. They would remember the lame leaping for joy, and the crowds shouting with excitement. But somehow, those memories would always sour for they would also remember that day on Dead Man's Hill. Peter could close his eyes even now and hear the sound of a hammer driving nails through human flesh. John would see the crown of thorns whenever he tried to sleep. James still winced when he remembered the curses and mockery of the crowd who watched Him die. Yes, they had their memories, but even memories are no comfort when they end on a cross.

Thus, these eleven men and a few women, all followers of a dead man, waited in a small upper room for God only knows what. Perhaps they were lonely; perhaps they were afraid the same thing would happen to them; perhaps they just didn't know what else to do. Sometimes they spoke, but mostly they just waited.

It was early in the morning on the first day of the week when Peter, John, and Mary were commissioned by the others to go to the tomb of Jesus and make the final preparations before the tomb would be sealed forever. Later, the crispness of the early morning air was filled with the shouts of Peter, John, and Mary as they ran to tell the others the Master had risen. On the night following, all of the disciples, save Thomas, were gathered again in the small upper room when Jesus came to them and blessed them. The next day one of the disciples, possibly James, went to find Thomas. When he found him, James' words tumbled out as water over a waterfall, "The Master has risen! He came back just as he said He would! We all saw Him, and talked to Him!"

A cynical smile crossed the face of Thomas before he spoke. "Unless I see in His hands the print of the nails, and place my finger in the mark of the nails, and place my hand in His side," he said, "I will not believe. However to satisfy my curiosity I will come with you. You need at least one rational man in your midst."

And so Thomas went with the rest of the disciples. Had you been there, and had you taken the time to observe the face of Thomas, you would have seen there a glimmer of hope which betrayed the cynicism. An hour passed into a day, and the day into a week. Thomas was just about ready to say to the others, "See, I told you so; He has not really risen. You have all been fools. You imagined the whole thing." But just at that moment Thomas heard the rustle of a tunic, and a great calm drifted over his body. He turned to look, and the sight brought him to his knees. It was the Master; His eyes surveyed the room and finally fell on Thomas. It was the kind of look which made Thomas feel ashamed.

The Master spoke, "Put your finger here, Thomas, and see my hands, and put out your hand and place it in my side. Do not be faithless but believing."

Tears streamed down the face of Thomas as through the sobs he cried, "My Lord and my God."

When I realized the truth and reality of the above incident, I realized there is a face to the future. I realized no matter how little is done by good men, or how much by evil men, God is still in charge. I realized He is sovereign; He controls the future; He has a plan, the fulfillment of which will bring history to an exciting and wonderful conclusion.

The resurrection of Christ, far from being only an isolated incident used by God to inspire belief, is a sign from God about man's future. If it really happened, and I believe it did, then the world is not the meaningless, absurd joke the existentialist would have us believe. If it really happened then God has not left us to our atomic toys. If it really happened then hope has been vindicated, and we can dream again.

Because Jesus Christ came back from the dead, we can say something about man's history. We can know history is not circular nor repetitive. It is moving toward God, at His pace, in His time. The history books record the past plan of God, not the plan of man. The civilizations which have passed from the face of the earth did so because they no longer would fit into God's plan. He is the Lord of history; He stands above history; history is His. How do I know? Because His sign was the resurrection. In the resurrection of Christ, God was saying to man that He was still in charge even when His own Son was hung on a cross.

Consider the time of the coming of Jesus Christ. Before His coming, there were two great streams of human history. There was the Jewish stream of history which carried with it the knowledge of a sovereign, personal God. This knowledge was held by a small group of wandering Jews who managed (contrary to the theories of any modern sociologist) to hold it firm against paganism and idolatry. It was guarded as a sacred trust. The other stream of history sprang from the Greeks and Romans. Within this stream of history, one finds great learning, art and literature, earthly power, and the ability to conquer, control, and build roads over almost all the known world. At only one time in the history of mankind did these streams come together, and it was in the first century A.D. For the first time, the whole world was ruled by one power. For the first time, there was a language which would communicate to everyman. For the first time, there were roads over which a message could be carried to the world. It was here God chose to bring man the revelation of His Son. It was here, in the first century, God chose to illustrate His love on a cross. Had Jesus Christ been born a hundred years before or a hundred years after the time of His actual coming, we would never have heard His name, and you would not be reading this book. Accident? Coincidence? Of course not! It was the plan of Him who controls history.

Consider the timing of the Apostle Paul's ministry, the Reformation, the Great Awakening, the great mission enterprises of the church. These were not accidents.

115

They were planned by God as He worked in history. History is not moving just anywhere. It is moving toward God and the end which God has planned. That end was described by Jesus Himself, "And then they will see the Son of man coming in a cloud with power and great glory" (Luke 21:17). After the followers of Jesus had seen the ascension of Christ, an angel told them, "Men of Galilee, why do you stand looking into heaven? This Jesus, who was taken up from you into heaven, will come in the same way as you saw him go into heaven" (Acts 1:11). Paul adds his testimony, "For the grace of God has appeared for the salvation of all men, training us to renounce irreligion and worldly passions, and to live sober, upright, and godly lives in this world, awaiting our blessed hope, the appearing of the great glory of our great God and Savior Jesus Christ ... " (Titus 2:11–13). No matter how big the bombs, how frightening the crises, nor how threatening the future, God is still in charge. His Son came back from the grave to tell us so.

The resurrection of Christ is also a sign which points to the future of the church. There are many reasons why I believe the church of Jesus Christ will not die, and I have discussed some of them in previous chapters. However, the central reason the church will not die is because the Head of the church is not dead. He promised " ... the powers of death shall not prevail" against His church. As long as He is alive, He will keep that promise.

How foolish we are to think the future of Christ's church depends on us. If it did, we would be in serious trouble. Our petty differences would weaken us, and our small efforts would destroy us. If the church depended on only men, we could take down our crosses and close

116

our doors. But the Rock upon which the church is built is not that fragile. The Rock triumphed over the cross and the grave. It will not collapse under the weight of the church. The church's one Foundation is Jesus Christ her Lord, and that is enough to insure her future.

Because Jesus Christ came back from the grave, we have a word to speak to the individual followers of Him. Most people, if you ask them, will tell you they believe in some kind of immortality. That belief may be a vague hope in the "good that lives after" or it may include streets of twenty-four karat gold, but whatever the belief, it expresses the wish that death will not stand victorious over life. The problem with belief in immortality is that very few people have any real basis for it. If our hope is grounded only in wishful thinking, it may comfort us, it may help us to sleep better at night, it may give us the strength to stand beside the graves of our loved ones, but we will only be fooling ourselves. Rose-colored glasses may make the world look better, but better color is in the glasses and not the world. Some people place their hope in the sign given us at spring. The flowers and the trees, they say, are reborn in the spring. The cycle is at the heart of things and therefore is applicable to me. Not so! The ultimate end of everything is death. The tree may be reborn many times within its life span, but finally it will rot and provide fertilizer for the soil which will bring forth new trees. (Trees have bark, but thus far, I have heard no one say we will also have bark.) A hope based in such faulty data is no more than a straw in the wind. There are those who seem to be content to place their hope in the ongoing of the human race. That which they contribute to the race will provide their immortality.

That has a poetic ring to it, but it doesn't mean much. It means even less when you are a part of the generation which knows it just may not be ongoing. Others say they believe in immortality because of the incompleteness of this life. They would see our incomplete knowledge, and incomplete skills, and incomplete ambitions as pointing to a place of completeness. It's not so, any more than the fact it rained in the middle of my golf game today should be the basis of a weather prediction about sunshine tomorrow. Others are willing to place their faith in the sermons of their favorite minister. But the fact of the matter is that ministers are going to die, too. They just don't know.

The only hope which is real springs from the living Christ. He is the only Man who has been there and come back to tell us about it. That we will die is a fact. The statistic is one out of one, and it is always the same. Our questions do not center around death but life, and the only place where we will find real answers is from the One who said, "I am the resurrection and the life; he who believes in me, though he die, yet shall he live, and whoever lives and believes in me shall never die" (John 11:25–26). If He really came back from the dead, then He knows what He is talking about. If He really came back from the dead, the morticians will not have the final say, the grave will have no victory, and death will have no sting.

The faith we profess stands or falls on the truth of the Resurrection of Christ. Paul said, "But if there is no resurrection of the dead, then Christ has not been raised; if Christ has not been raised, then our preaching is in vain and your faith is in vain" (I Corinthians 15:13–14).

The great fact of history is that Jesus Christ is alive. Because of that fact our history is purposeful, our church is deathless, and our life is forever. Hallelujah!

"These all died in faith, not having received what was promised..." (Hebrews 11:13). Chew on that, those of you who feel that the Bible is unrealistic. The flaw of human existence is the fact of unfulfilled promises. The Bible understands that fact and is honest about it. Moses worked for forty years to lead his people to a land "flowing with milk and honey." And when the promise was almost fulfilled, he was led up on a mountain where his old eyes were allowed to view the Promised Land. But Moses died on that mountain. The goal for which he had worked and prayed so long was unrealized for him. The Bible tells it as it is: "These all died in faith, not having received what was promised...."

The prophet Isaiah lived in the hope of a coming Messiah who would redeem Israel. Tears must have streamed down his face as he brought forth the word of his God. "Surely he has borne our griefs and carried our sorrows; yet we esteemed him stricken, smitten by God and afflicted. But he was wounded for our transgressions, he was bruised for our iniquities; upon him was the chastisement that made us whole, and with his stripes we are healed. All we like sheep have gone astray; we have turned every one to his own way; and the Lord has laid on him the iniquity of us all" (Isaiah 53:4–6). How wonderful if Isaiah could have seen the Messiah he described so beautifully in his book. But Isaiah died nearly seven hundred years before the Messiah came. "These all died in faith, not having received what was promised...."

The Apostle Paul had a dream of preaching the Gospel to the world. He wrote to the church at Rome, "I hope to see you in passing as I go to Spain" (Romans 15:24). The Gospel preached to a people who lived beyond the place where any Christian has ever gone before. How exciting! But Paul didn't make Spain. He had his head chopped off in Rome. "These all died in faith, not having received what was promised. . . . "

Jesus said the merciful are blessed; He said they would be shown mercy. But I have seen the merciful called suckers. I have seen them used by the world as an object of derision. Jesus said those who were hungry for righteousness would be filled. But a man told me yesterday that more than anything he wanted to be different. "Steve," he said, "I try every day of my life, and I fail every day of my life." Unfulfilled promises are a fact of life. When a telegram is opened and a tear falls on the words, "Missing in action . . . ," when children realize their parents have made serious mistakes, when men labor for a lifetime without result, the words of the Bible once again bring home the sad but true fact that "these all died in faith, not having received what was promised. . . . "

But the good news of Christ is that there is a future where books are always balanced. It is a future ruled by One who knows each tear and hurt. It is a future where God always writes a happy ending. It isn't pie in the sky either. It is true and wonderful. Listen, "These all died in faith, not having received what was promised. . . . Therefore God is not ashamed to be called their God, for he has prepared for them a city" (Hebrews 11:16). That is the good news about the future to those who believe.

In the future there is justification for the Christian who must suffer for his faith. The man or woman who claims allegiance to Jesus Christ is a threat to those who claim allegiance to lesser gods. Because the Christian refuses to buy what the world is selling—its hate, its blasé sophistication, its goals—the world will bring out its cross. Oh, it's not a wooden cross anymore. That just isn't civilized. Laughter and words are better because they prolong the pain of destruction. Jesus understands the price many Christians pay for their faith. His words speak to the condition: "Blessed are you when man revile you and persecute you and utter all kinds of evil against you falsely on my account. Rejoice and be glad, for your reward is great in heaven, for so men persecuted the prophets who were before you" (Matthew 5:11–12).

The future belongs to Jesus Christ. In that future He will be victorious. "Gentle Jesus, meek and mild" won't be so gentle, so meek, nor so mild in the future. The "King of kings" won't hang on a cross again! The next time it will be a throne before which will be gathered all the nations. He will call His own, and they will hear His voice, and all men will know His power. "Therefore God has highly exalted him and bestowed on him the name which is above every name, that at the name of Jesus every knee should bow, in heaven and on earth and under the earth, and every tongue confess that Jesus Christ is Lord, to the glory of God the Father" (Philippians 2:9–11). That is the good news (or bad news, depending on your perspective) about the future.

Recently, a man said to me, "Young man, I can't understand why you decided to be a minister. You will be out of business soon. People don't need religion anymore." I don't know the reason for the man's words. Perhaps he was expressing a hurt which needed to be healed. Perhaps he was looking for an ultimate and had been discouraged when he sought it in the church. But on the chance he was really looking for information, I would like to say some things now that were not appropriate then.

First, I am in the ministry because I have given my future to Jesus Christ, and that is where He wanted me. When I gave Him my future, I got the best end of the deal. I traded in an uncertain future loaded with anxiety and boredom. He took that future, filled it with meaning and gave it back to me. I gave Him my chains, and He gave me my freedom. The trade was sealed on a cross and validated with an empty tomb. Sometimes, on Monday morning, when the organ is silenced for another week, when there are no hands to shake, and no youth to inspire, I want to forget about the trade. Sometimes, on Monday morning, when I sit down before the notes of a sermon which didn't quite make it, I want to run away. When I have to explain to a mother there is nothing more the doctors can do for her child, when I spend a night trying to help a drunk with the D.T.'s dry out, when a young man's wife is killed in a tragic automobile accident and he asks me, "Why?" I want to turn away and cry. But I'm in the ministry to stay because a "strange Man on a cross" won't let me leave.

I believe God has a plan for every person. Most people don't follow that plan, but it is still there. Jesus Christ calls people to the future. He has a place for all those who would hear and accept that call. Some who hear the call are sent into the world of business, and others are sent home to become the "home anchor." Some are called to serve in government, communications, or science. Others are given a trade, and some are told to teach. All of His followers are a part of His future. I am, too. That's why I am a minister.

I am a minister because I realized, as Thomas Chalmers put it, two magnitudes: the shortness of time and the vastness of eternity. One of those magnitudes without the other would have kept me out of the ministry. Were time not short, the importance of what one does with time would be diminished. One could do many things and have time to do them all; one could dilly-dally, and it wouldn't really matter much. But time is short. Job understood the shortness of time when he said, "Man that is born of a woman is of few days, and full of trouble. He comes forth like a flower, and withers; he flees like a shadow, and continues not" (Job 14:1–2). That is true, and because it is true, a man must consider carefully the work to which he will give himself. It is in the ministry that I can best point to things which really matter. In the ministry I have found God's place for me to spend the life He has given in a way which will cause me to say when I have come to the end of my time, "I have fought the good fight, I have finished the race, I have kept the faith. Henceforth there is laid up for me the crown of righteousness, which the Lord, the righteous judge, will award to me on that Day, and not only to me but also to all who have loved his appearing" (II Timothy 4:7–8).

But there is another magnitude. It is the vastness of

eternity. Someone has said there is an election going on all the time. The Lord casts a vote for you, the devil casts a vote against you, and you cast the deciding vote. The vote I cast wouldn't matter much were it not for the vastness of eternity. Thomas à Kempis writes in *The Imitation of Christ*, "Very quickly there will be an end of thee here; look what will become of thee in another world. Today man is; and tomorrow he appeareth not. And when he is taken away from the eyes, quickly also he passeth out of mind. O dullness and hardness of man's heart, which thinketh only upon the present, and doth not rather care for what is to come!"

If it were not for the vastness of eternity, I would probably have given myself to getting for myself. Perhaps there would have been more money. Perhaps I could have had a nicer house and a bigger insurance policy, and then I would die, my life having been only a pleasant interlude between two states of nonexistence. But it isn't that way. Jesus told about a man who had everything. He got up one morning and looked out on his farm lands, and he thought to himself, "I've got it made. I have so much that I don't have any place to put it. I'm going to put all my land in soil-bank and I am going to sit down, pat myself on the back, and spend the rest of my time eating, drinking and making merry." But Jesus said God said to that man, "Fool! This night your soul is required of you; and the things you have prepared, whose will they be?" (Luke 12:16–21). I am a minister because I have understood the shortness of time and the vastness of eternity.

I am also in the ministry because I have something extremely important to share. I don't claim to be a religious oracle giving divine truth to those who will listen. When I met Jesus, He didn't give me a superior intellect; He didn't make me the receiver of all His truth; I didn't escape the necessity of much growth and many failures. As Karl Barth writes in *The Faith of the Church,* "It is important that we take the Church seriously. But we must not take ourselves too seriously as ministers. Do not fancy that in your parish you are God's angel with the flaming sword! You are just a simple minister permitted to preach the good news. Be sure that there are other "angels" (that is, messengers) than you! They may be very odd angels, but they are angels! Tell yourself: I will do my best but at the same time I know that the coming of the Kingdom does not depend on me. It is not I who ought to accomplish everything. ... My manse is not a little island of peace and justice in a sea of injustice." No, I was not given the ability to give forth God's Word as dictated to me, but I'll tell you what I was given. I was given a real experience of Jesus Christ. Because of Him, I know why I'm here, who I am and where I am going, and I can't keep quiet about it. Charles Wesley's experience is mine:

> My heart is full of Christ, and longs
> Its glorious matter to declare!
> Of Him I make my loftier psalms,
> I cannot from His praise forbear;
> My ready tongue makes haste to sing
> The glories of my heavenly King.

Finally, I am a minister for very selfish reasons. I think that often ministers give the impression they are the most unhappy and unappreciated people in the world. We spend a lot of time complaining about the low salary, the big cold manse, and the demanding parishioners. However, that is just the propaganda we put out to confuse those who have a tendency to believe we "work only an hour a week with a month to rest from that." You see, it makes me feel good when someone tells me how committed I am to give up so much to serve the church. I like people to think I have made great sacrifices to enter the ministry. My ego grows each time someone pats me on the back and says, "Reverend, you must love the Lord very much." Well, I have decided to reveal all! Herewith is the plain, uncensored truth. The ministry is the greatest life going.

Where else can a man have time to read the books which most interest him, to sit down and talk to his friends without always having another appointment, to perform his task without having to punch a clock? There is no other profession in the world which gives a man so much freedom to fulfill his task. Of course, the minister had better use the time that is given him wisely, lest, when the people gather to worship on the Sabbath, he has nothing to tell them. Gerald Kennedy quotes the words of William Quayle when he tells this story in *With Singleness of Heart*. "When this preacher comes to a Sunday in his journey through the week, people ask him, 'Preacherman, where were you and what saw you while the workdays were sweating at their toil?' And then of this preacher we may say reverently, 'He opened his mouth and taught them, saying: "And there will be another though lesser Sermon on the Mount." And the auditors sit and sob and shout under their breath, and say with their helped hearts, 'Preacher, saw you and heard you that? You were well employed. Go out and listen and look another week; but be very sure to come back and tell us what you heard and saw.' That will be preaching."

The ministry is the greatest life going because it is here a man can meet his fellowmen where they are really living. A minister probably knows more people intimately—their joys, sorrows, loves, and disappointment—than anyone else. He is given access to hundreds of lives that would be closed to anyone else. He is there when a baby is born; he shares the heartache of growing up. When love blossoms and a couple decide to become one, it is the minister who is given the privilege of guidance and the honor of bestowing the church's blessing. When death cuts into life, it is the minister who is allowed to comfort and speak the words of Christ. Someone once told me a man was lucky to have as many as two real friends in a lifetime. If that is true, then I am richly blessed.

The ministry is a great place to be when you consider the love and understanding of the laymen. I have had some seminary professors who at least implied the minister's job was to "do battle with the laymen." Sometimes a young minister is given the impression that whenever he tries to do anything new or creative or different, he will run up against the narrowness and intransigence of the laymen. That just isn't true. It is just an excuse some would use to cover their failure. Most laymen in the church are just waiting for their minister to take the first step (some have decided he never will, and have gone out on their own). When I think, in just the short time I have been a minister, of the men and women who have corrected me in love and have praised me with pride, I thank God that He has put me where I am.

Finally, I have given my future to the ministry because I

have the privilege of seeing men and women come under the power and influence of Jesus Christ. Gerald Kennedy speaks about this joy, "There is no joy to compare with the evangelist's. A man never loses the happiness of his calling if he is winning men to Christ. He can put up with many disappointments and go through many a sore trial without surrender if he is introducing men to his Lord. . . . We were not meant to be promoters or administrators or purchasing agents, though we must do something in each of these fields. We were meant to be bringers of good tidings to disappointed men."

There is great joy when men and women come to know Jesus Christ. It is all the more wonderful for me if I have had a hand in the introduction. Because people call me "Reverend," they expect me to have something to say about God. That kind of opportunity is afforded to few people. If one has something to say—and I do—then what a great privilege! Can you imagine? Having all of this and getting paid for it!

If the Lord tarries, I believe that the next fifty years will be the most exciting years in the history of the church. The Holy Spirit is once again stirring among the people of God. God is setting the stage for a mighty work. I am young. I am a minister. I will live during those years. I'm glad.